LOWI & G

LIVING OUTSIDE THE LINES

Lori Brown & Angela Miller Barton

Big Words Publishing

Copyright © 2017 by Lori Brown and Angela Miller Barton

www.LowiandG.com

Published 2017

Editor: Heather Doyle Fraser
Cover Design by Danielle Baird
Book Design by Danielle Baird
Lori Brown Author Photo by Becca Howard, Free Spirit Colorado
Anglea Miller Barton Author Photo by Catherine Murray

Printed in the United States of America

ISBN-13: 978-0-692-89429-3

First Edition

Big Words Publishing — Dublin, Ohio
www.BigWordsPublishing.com

For Andy, Alexandra, Sydney and Reese.
I love you always.

For John.

TABLE OF CONTENTS

PART 3—NOT WHAT I WAS EXPECTING

PART 4—KICKING AND SCREAMING TOWARDS GRATITUDE

PART 5—WHERE'S MY MAP?

PART 6—ARE WE THERE YET?

LOWI & G

INTRODUCTION: BEING LOWI & G

*"So, I guess we are who we are for a lot of reasons.
And maybe we'll never know most of them. But even
if we don't have the power to choose where we come
from, we can still choose where we go from there."*

—Stephen Chbosky, *The Perks of Being a Wallflower*

We're Lowi and G. Already you may be asking if our parents were under the "influence" or partaking in some "recreational substance" upon naming us. While we can't rule that out, Lowi and G come from some of the great relationships we have in life. These are the names we have inherited from our nieces.

In our regular lives, we are Lori and Angela.

Lori's daughters gave Angela the name G. And our niece, Ava, rounded out the nicknames with Lowi for Lori (as in LO-EE). While they've grown up, and thankfully their language skills are much better, the loving monikers have remained.

We are sisters by chance, and friends by choice. We are sarcastic, striving, and struggling zen masters.

From our small-town roots to fitfully building unconfined lives we've maintained similar hopes and goals. We are committed to happiness, fulfillment, feeling good enough, getting help, and helping others. We are all about living better, but we may possibly have an overdeveloped sarcastic side.

We strongly believe that our place in the world—dysfunction junction—is being inhabited by many of you as well. And it's time to say it, own it, and get a laugh out of it. We are knee-deep in this road trip of life and the map was blown out the window many dirt-road miles ago. We are stumbling toward living genuinely open and real. We like to do that with a healthy dose of sarcasm. At times it helps to make the pills go down more smoothly, and then in other situations, it gets in the way of living more authentically and joyfully. So we balance on the beam between these two forces, ready to catch ourselves, leaning in to one side or the other whenever necessary.

We strive to say yes to those things that force us to choose between the well-worn path and the one less traveled; to leap face first into the unknown; to choose love and laughter over sadness and fear. While we embrace the bite and cunning of sarcasm, we also take time to bask in the vulnerable joys of sunshine. We traffic in the rawness of life, truth and then chase it with forays into gratitude, redemption, and a shot of laughter.

After years of dreaming of doing a project together we finally launched a blog Lowi & G: For People Who Appreciate Sunshine and Sarcasm (http://lowiandg.com), and now this book. And here's a funny thing—when you decide to start writing and publishing your work for the whole world to see, you really find yourself pondering some deep questions, "Who am I?" And then that question gets morphed into, "Which part of me am I going to show the world?" and then that can become, "Who do I want the world to think I am?" And that's where we get into trouble.

Sometimes these thoughts and questions can start to feel complicated: who am I, who do I want the world to think I am, how can I be me and reflect positively on my sister as well? And as you can imagine, it's a nearly endless circle of the drain. Luckily, when you're writing with your sister you have a partner in these circles and you can remind each other:

#1: WE HAVE SOMETHING TO SAY.

#2: SOMETIMES TO BE REAL YOU HAVE TO BE RAW.

And in the end, all this questioning, all this circling turned out to be a jumping off point—not off the cliff—a beginning to a conversation that we all need to have. Even if it's just with ourselves.

We all are trying to figure it out:

Who am I?

Who do I want to be?

And how is that different than who I am with my spouse, friends, family, co-workers, acquaintances?

There are times in our lives—even right now—where there are people from whom we hide our true selves. We don't quite let them see who we are. Instead, we try to be who we think they want us to be. In these moments we feel less than genuine. We feel like liars. And sometimes, that line between when you are pretending to be someone else and when you are being yourself gets blurry. And pretty soon, pretending starts to feel easier.

Being vulnerable enough to be seen, even in the most basic sense, can be tough.

While we may not let our freak flag fly quite so openly with someone we just met that doesn't mean we can't still be ourselves. As Brené Brown says, "Only some people have earned the right to hear our stories." But at the same time, we can be the essence of ourselves with everyone.

This is how we do life and when we get to the other side of our "dash" we want to be skidding in, barely making it under the wire and for God to look at us and say, "Glad you could make it, I thought you might be here sooner, but at least you made it."

We hope this collection of stories and missteps of our lives gives you lots of reasons to laugh, courage to tackle one of your goals, and a sense of belonging if you feel like you don't fit in everywhere else.

This is our story told in the only way we can—sunshine & sarcasm.

Welcome to Lowi & G.

THE RULES

"To every rule there is an exception—and an idiot
ready to demonstrate it. Don't be the one!"

— Vera Nazarian, *The Perpetual Calendar of Inspiration*

LOWI
&G

THE PROPER CARE AND FEEDING OF SARCASM

"I try not to break the rules but merely to test their elasticity."

—Bill Veeck

The salty and snarky of sarcasm doesn't come without its rules. I am not sure if these are universal or only exist in our minds, but there are, in fact, boundaries.

RULE #1 SARCASM IS ALWAYS GOOD IN A CRISIS.

When tensions are running high and you don't know how things are going to go, a well-played sarcastic comment can help out.

If you are looking for a how-to on this, it goes something like:

Your dad is in the hospital for surgery and while sitting in the waiting room your mom talks about how tired she is because she was awake all night. Then adds earnestly, "Usually not sleeping isn't a problem for me."

You artfully add, "Hmm, you're right. It is weird that you need sleep unlike the rest of us humans..."

Glare given, glare received, but the tension is broken.

RULE #2 — SARCASM IS OFTEN A GOOD ICE-BREAKER AND FRIEND-MAKER.

As a yoga teacher, I often have new people in class and they can be nervous. They have all these scenarios rolling around in their head about what yoga is, will be, and what I will make them do. So I often try to add a little ice-breaker to let them know things are OK.

We sit down and everyone dutifully tries to put themselves into lotus position. I usually jump in and remind the class that they can sit with their legs folded or legs extended. Then I offer, "If you have your legs folded and you are wondering, 'Dear God, how long will we sit like this?' then extending your legs might be a better choice." This is also a great way to let them know that smiling is allowed in yoga—at least in my yoga class.

RULE # 3 — IT'S OFTEN BEST IN A "IF YOU DIDN'T LAUGH, YOU'D CRY" SITUATION.

When you have played sports and your kids play sports you tend not to get too excited about small injuries and ailments. So when my oldest was in sixth grade and she complained of a jammed thumb after a volleyball game I told her to suck it up. The next morning her entire arm was swollen to her elbow. On the verge of a breakdown, I made an emergency appointment. When the orthopedist said she would be casted for six weeks and possibly need surgery I sheepishly asked, "So, you are saying I am a shoo-in for mother of the year?"

RULE # 4 — IT MAKES THE HARD DAYS EASIER.

On some of the toughest of days, when your positivity toolbox isn't equipped for what you are going through, sometimes sarcasm is just what you need. It's a witty little beast and it can give you the edge you need to get through the day.

Like following a funeral when tensions were running high, our aunt started to show red-zone-dog qualities toward another relation. Instead of letting things get heated and feeding the frenzy, Lowi suggested to her sassily that if she couldn't keep it together we might need to "leash her."

It can be just the right note to turn things around. In this moment, our aunt laughed and let out a bark.

RULE # 5 — SARCASM CAN TAKE THE STING OUT OF WHAT NEEDS SAYING.

Sometimes we all need a reality check. We need to leave our first-world problems at the door and get grounded. But, on occasion, we just aren't getting there on our own.

Instead of telling someone that they are being self-centered, idiotic or a whole host of other unkind things, you can use your sarcastic super powers for good and help the other person save face.

When your friend is going on and on about how her order was messed up at Starbucks, you can slyly say, "OMG you're right. How ever will you go on? Maybe we should hire a hitman for the barista before any more senseless acts of mistaken coffees hit the world."

Dramatic? Yes. A little snarky? Also, yes. A little nicer than, "Shut up, already." I think, yes!

RULE #6 BE WARNED, SARCASM IS MUCH LIKE GREMLINS.

It doesn't do well in bright light.

One of the sharp corners of sarcasm, is that it doesn't play well with Pollyanna. I know we're all about sunshine, but we're down with real, true goodness. The fake, polished, nonsensical happy, happy, happy tends to bring out the grittier side of our sarcasm. It's possible that at certain times we need to rein it in.

It's best not to feed and encourage sarcasm after dark or cocktails unless you're certain your shared company is playing from the same deck. Otherwise you're Strip Poker and they are Go Fish. You see where I am going?

Once at a party, a guy I just met was going on and on about how hard it was for him to follow a Paleo diet when out to dinner. It seemed rather over the top and in an effort to add a little levity, I commented, "How hard is it to run into a dead cow at a restaurant?"

A little too late I realized they were playing Old Maid and I, on the other hand, just pulled from Cards Against Humanity.

I wasn't invited back.

RULE # 7 SARCASM IS THE LITMUS TEST THAT DOESN'T LIE.

If the person you're with doesn't appreciate sarcasm, keep moving.

While in college, I worked at the student newspaper with a guy named Tony. I used to give him a hard time and lots of sarcastic jabs. He followed suit and offered up the same. One day someone asked why he was so sarcastic and he replied, "I kid 'cause I care." Needless to say, if you can't play the sarcasm game, we won't bother you with it. But it might also be our sign to keep moving on down the road.

LOWI & G

THE PROPER CARE AND FEEDING OF SUNSHINE

"Three simple rules in life: If you do not go after what you want, you'll never have it. If you do not ask, the answer will always be no. If you do not step forward, you will always be in the same place."

— Anonymous

The warm brightness of sunshine also has its rules of engagement. Despite popular belief you can't just throw those rays anywhere.

RULE # 1 SUNSHINE IS ALWAYS GOOD IN A CRISIS.

Albeit difficult to admit, some situations are too far gone for sarcasm. Blasphemy? Not quite.

Well-played sunshine can give just what is needed. When our aunt was in the hospital recovering from major surgery a few nights were brutally rough. When you're scared, in pain, and more than a little exhausted, what you need is a light to look forward to. So we talked about vacation planning. Now, she was seriously drugged so I did most of the planning, but dawn arrived faster and everything looked better in the light of day while thinking about the beach.

RULE # 2 — SUNSHINE IS OFTEN A GOOD ICE-BREAKER AND FRIEND-MAKER.

On a particularly cold and difficult day at a race, I stumbled upon a fellow runner who was having a tough time. I slowed and talked with her a bit and we got through the next couple miles in what felt like no time at all. We saw each other here and there along the course the rest of the day. About 30 hours after the race, I received a Facebook friend request from her and we've been virtual buddies for nearly three years. All thanks to a smile and some Gatorade.

RULE # 3 IT'S OFTEN BEST IN A "IF YOU DIDN'T LAUGH, YOU'D CRY" SITUATION.

Lowi and I found ourselves in an awkward funeral situation. We were trapped chatting it up with an overly friendly attendee. We made eye contact many times during this exchange and just laughed and put on our warmest, sun-shiniest faces because otherwise there most certainly would've been tears. Well, maybe not tears, but possibly eye-rolling, sighing or cringing.

RULE # 4 IT MAKES THE HARD DAYS EASIER.

After a particularly difficult trip with some work colleagues, we were on our way home and delayed at the airport. We were physically tired, emotionally tired, and more than a little ready to just get home. We talked about our "must-do" lists and all the things we really enjoyed. When two of my co-travelers, who are nervous flyers, suggested we hold hands for takeoff, we did because it made everyone feel better. The rays of light felt warm even in the dark of a rainy night.

RULE # 5 — SUNSHINE CAN TAKE THE STING OUT OF WHAT NEEDS SAYING.

Much like Southerners say, "Bless Your Heart," when they think you've done lost your mind, sunshine can go a long way in swallowing the bitter pill of truth. A friend of mine often talks about her Born-Again Pentecostal hairdresser who, when about to throw down some knowledge, tells her he "speaks the truth in love." That's just how sunshine works in taking the sting out of the truth-filled bee. Say it, say it with love, say it with kindness, but for God's sake, say it.

RULE # 6 — BE WARNED, SUNSHINE IS MUCH LIKE GIZMO.

Nobody likes fake or, "bright light, bright light!" If your warm and positive disposition is an act, please revert directly to sarcasm. It'll play better, you'll be more sincere, maybe elicit a laugh and keep your retinas intact. That's sunshine, right?

RULE #7 SUNSHINE IS THE LITMUS TEST THAT DOESN'T LIE.

When you meet someone who has an issue with sunshine at every turn, it's important to put on your sunglasses and back away slowly. You don't want to make any sudden movements around these kind. They're jumpy and more than a little sketchy. If someone doesn't like your brand of sunshine, it's cool, but don't waste it on them either.

I used to work with a woman who found my overall disposition to be annoying. Try as I might, when I was nice she was annoyed and when I was indifferent she was annoyed. Pretty soon I was annoyed, too. When I stopped trying to share my style of sunshine with her, life got a whole lot better. At least for me. I don't know how her life was, she didn't talk to me—and that was totally OK by me.

PART 1

ROOTS

"It takes courage to grow up and become who you really are."

— e. e. cummings

HOMETOWN

"The nice part about living in a small town is that when you don't know what you are doing, someone else does."

—Immanuel Kant

Regularly and often I run from my hometown. I don't want to claim it, and I sure as hell don't want it to claim me.

The reality is, I am a small town girl.

I was raised in a village with three traffic lights, two of which blinked after 10:00 p.m. You could speed through certain parts of town as long as you were a local, and Friday nights were for football.

We grew up going to a cement brick church on Sundays. It was as plain and simple as you imagine... maybe more.

With folding chairs, a piano, and traditional gender roles in place, it was everything you might expect from a small town church. And in towns like these, progress and change come slow, if at all. In the nearly two decades I attended this church it held tight to tradition and there wasn't much fluctuation. On the occasion now that I attend with my parents, who are still members, it appears much is the same. The same baritone is leading the hymns, the congregation is made up of the same core families, and it likely will remain just that—the same.

A small town is not unlike a family. It has its own moral code and social mores. And if you don't fall within those standards there are repercussions. Not all of them serious, but deviation never goes unnoticed. And that's just how it is.

Being small town is what we know and it's comfortable in a sense, even if we haven't been part of the community in decades. There are many things right about a small town: You're family whether you're blood or not. They never forget you, and even if you try, you don't forget them.

That's how much of our formative years were shaped in claustrophobic belonging—it pulled us in as grade-schoolers and made us feel safe. As we aged, though, that same quality threatened our dreams and could've anchored us where we stood.

When you are a small town girl there is an unrelenting tug of war that's waged for your soul.

Leave or stay. Belong or be on the outside. There is no halfway.

But at home it was clearer. While we were growing up, our mom had two unflagging imperatives:

1. GO TO COLLEGE.
2. LEAVE THIS TOWN.

Like good small town girls, we followed her rules; however, Lowi took leaving town more seriously, as she's several states away. I'm a mere 30 minutes outside of town (although there is a wanderlust inside that begs for attention).

Our mom had direct instructions, but what I heard was: Go out and do different things, be different.

We did and we are. And yet we remain forever tethered to this small stretch of Route 40. It's unchangeably home and while many other things have changed, this likely never will.

It's who we are.

SLEDDING

"Our best decisions, the ones we never regret,
come from listening to ourselves."

—Anonymous

Go-karts, snowmobiles, sledding hills, chili, and fighting over who could stand on the ONE furnace vent at my grandparents' house. These were some of my favorite things growing up. In fact, one very early Christmas morning, I can remember calling my grandparents at 5:30 a.m. to tell them that Santa had brought us snowmobile suits! It was just that important; we had to have the appropriate winter gear to hang with the cousins.

One memory that has stuck with me for years though is of a day sledding with the aunts, uncles, and cousins. Getting to the hill was half the fun as we were towed by a snowmobile on a large toboggan. It truly was like the song, "Over the river and through the woods to grand-mother's house we go..." I can remember the sledding hill seemed so large at the time, but in reality it is such a baby hill that I am embarrassed of how terrified I was back then. Having stood at the top of many black diamond ski hills in Colorado, I now know real terror.

The toboggan held four of us comfortably. There was my cousin Julie (affectionately known as Jube), my sister G, my Aunt Lisa, and myself.

There we were, our four small, scared selves teetering at the top of the mountain...I mean hill, and we were ready to go. Someone gave us a count of three and then a big shove (probably our Uncle Bobby because he has always gotten a sick, twisted sense of joy out of striking fear in young children). Halfway down the hill we saw the icy creek below and we bailed off that toboggan so fast we practically gave ourselves whiplash!

There was yelling and swearing and arms waving as we picked our little bodies up off the snow. The family was so disappointed in us. They wanted to know why we bailed so early. Hmmmm, I don't know because we didn't want to die in the icy creek perhaps? They gave us a talking to and promptly put us back on the toboggan at the top of the hill for round two with strict instructions: DO NOT BAIL.

Once again, we were pushed down the hill, and as the creek loomed large—we bailed. There were more tears and more assurances that we would naturally come to a stop well before the creek gobbled us up.

We were told,

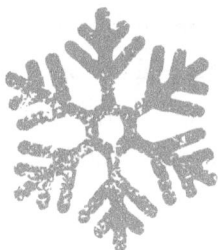

"DO NOT BAIL UNDER ANY CIRCUMSTANCES! YOU WILL BE FINE!"

So, with deep breaths and perhaps a blood pact (even though we were already related by blood, this was serious business when most of us were under the age of 7) we wrapped our little legs around the one in front of us and held tight. We would not fail...I mean bail. We would see this all the way through.

We passed the halfway mark, the sled went faster, the creek grew larger, and we held strong. As we approached the end of the snow and the drop off to the creek we could hear yelling. Oh, we would not fail this time. We would not bail. Then something like flight or fight took over as our young little lives began to pass before our eyes and in one swift movement we all bailed at the very last second.

The family came running, their arms were flailing and they were screaming something at us. I think it went something like this, "What were you thinking? Why did you wait so long to bail? Did you not see the creek? You scared the hell out of us! Do you want to do it again?"

All of these years I have thought of this story as just another day of sledding with the cousins. Perhaps it was the near-death experience, but it's not like our lives weren't in peril every time we rode on the back of a snowmobile with an uncle! Maybe it was because that was the day we found our courage.

We believed them when they said we would stop before we died in the icy abyss. OK, it's unlikely we would have actually died. I am sure they would have fished our helpless little bodies out of the creek and rushed us back to grandma's to stand over THE VENT! But, at the last moment we stopped listening to the voices and we made a choice to save ourselves.

LOWI
&G

BALD EAGLE

"Mothers are all slightly insane."

—J. D. Salinger

S ome people blossom from their cocoons into butterflies and still others are forced into transformation and emerge—a bald eagle.

G and I both escaped our small town roots, but not without a few titles to our name. I know you are probably thinking we are boasting about our accolades, but lest you get too judgmental, our titles consisted of things like "Little Miss Ox Roast Queen." Must I say more? I mean with a title like "Ox" attached to your name, you can never escape completely unscathed.

There are moments in our lives that leave an indelible mark. July 4, 1976, the Bicentennial Celebration, was one of those occasions. The moment in the making began several days before. I was young so I can only remember snapshots like how the pantyhose fit over my bushy brown hair and how hot it was.

I remember the very small pieces of gold tissue paper that were painstakingly glued to the cut-out poster board that would become my wings. I wanted to help with the wings, but my aunt had a plan, and I was not part of it. When you are 6 years old you can't always see the pattern of the would-be feathers.

I was to be entered in the best costume category of our Independence Day Celebration. I was a brown and gold bald eagle! (Coincidentally, these are also the town's school colors.) It's OK to laugh here. It's funny.

I also remember my mom working on my sister G's Little Miss Fourth of July dress. It was red, white, and blue and had short sleeves. It was lightweight and so pretty in my 6-year-old eyes. My outfit was brown and gold and ugly! Why did I have to be the American Bald Eagle and did it really have to be the town's colors? Why did I have to wear those pantyhose on my head? My hair was already short and brown!

The plan was for us to march in the annual parade. G was entered into the Little Miss Fourth of July portion and I was in the costume portion. G didn't want to walk because it was hot and she was 2 years old. It was my job to hold her hand and make sure she didn't chase a rogue baton or a random piece of candy left along the road.

I don't remember enjoying the parade. Even at this young age, I already knew that this outfit was not cool. This was not going to help my status in first grade, I mean I already had a kid who bit me every day in kindergarten.

The parade route ended in the park where awards would be given for best float, best costume, and, of course, Little Miss Fourth of July. I remember wanting to take my wings, my beak or at least my headdress off, but alas the judges might be watching and tallying votes. I didn't see any other costumes. There was only one other homely looking girl vying for Little Miss Fourth of July. I can say this because I was the most hideous specimen in the running for whatever was up for grabs.

Speaking of what was at stake, I remember a lot of hushed discussion going on with the judges and looks. I was sure that they were discussing how sad they were for me being a bald eagle and all.

I couldn't have been more wrong. They were discussing the fact that there were only three children in the running for all of the categories. Their brilliant idea was to combine Little Cutie Patootie G, the homely girl, and the bald eagle into one category and then vote. Really? Can anyone feel my pain right now? I mean what chance does a bald eagle have in the Little Miss Category? I think the answer has something to do with a snowball. Who in their right mind would vote for a kid dressed in a brown turtleneck, brown tights, brown pantyhose over their head, and a beak?

You know where this is going...

Yep G won Little Miss Fourth of July, the homely girl won second place and the Great American Bald Eagle won third place. Surprise!

Let me just say, that I am not bitter. In fact, this story has brought much laughter to those around me for decades. Right here I would like to give a big shout out to my friends in book club with whom I shared this story in confidence.

Two weeks later, I received an unmarked box in the mail. Inside was a brown and gold bald eagle.

Yep, it's the moment that just keeps on giving. Thanks, Mom.

THREE TREES
AND COUNTLESS TEENS

*"I didn't know I had OCD until I watched my kids
hang ornaments on the tree wherever they wanted."*

—Simon Holland

For many, traditions begin with a sacred significance or desire to mark a special event. One of our favorite holiday traditions though may have evolved more out of simple Christmas tree envy than complex sanctity.

Sometime during my middle school years we began decorating our parents' house for Christmas with a group of friends. It began as an extension of our days at the Christmas Tree Festival. I remember my mom used to drag us downtown to see hundreds of trees decorated in different themes. Every theme you can imagine was on display from monochromatic white-flocked

trees to trees all decked out in trains. I mean these people went all out!

Somewhere along the line my mom and her flock
of children and neighborhood kids became inspired to
go home and replicate the holiday spirit that they wit-
nessed at this festival. Hence the Christmas Decorating
Party was born.

Looking back, I think our mom really just wanted that white tree with powder blue decorations, but
she ended up with much more than she bargained for.
Each year, there were more and more kids, and during
my college years it culminated into a Christmas slumber party.

The chaos and joy that ensued each year regular-
ly coincided with the Ohio State/Michigan game so
during college the party could not begin until the game
was over. But once the Buckeyes brought home a win,
the party began.

First, there was food. Anyone who knows our mother knows that she can cook and bake like no other.
In fact, that may have been the draw for many of our
friends. There would always be sloppy joes, Bev Cake,
as many of our friends referred to our mother's cakes
(for those of you new to the scene, our mother had her
own bakery), cookies of every kind, and as the evening
wore on we ordered pizza.

It was my dad's job to take a contingent of kids to find the perfect Christmas tree. Not an easy task, but I know he loved it. His favorite part? I am pretty sure my friend, who shall remain nameless, who referred to him as Tom Selleck, boosted his ego just a little bit each year.

After bringing the tree home and placing it in the prescribed corner, my dad would step back and let the games begin. While we were out picking the perfect tree, my mom was busy making fresh popcorn and lots of it. No good Christmas Decorating Party would be complete without stringing popcorn. In fact, there were a few that competed for this event each year. No where else would you find six-foot male athletes with needle and thread in hand competing for who could "sew" the longest strand of popcorn. Now those were good times!

You might be thinking that it sounds like a lot of kids for one tree, but alas, my mom had three trees. The live tree was the only one that didn't come with an instruction manual. There was one in the foyer that had certain specifications, but the instructions were easy to follow. The white tree was a different story. It's possible at one time there may have been auditions for decorating the white tree. This was mom's tree and not just anyone could partake in this sacred ornamentation. Lights and ornaments had to be placed correctly or Mom would have to do it herself.

Imagine, if you will, my mom and her advanced decorating class standing around the white tree with delicate ornaments while downstairs, popcorn was being ground into the carpet as we munched on sloppy joes, pizza, and cookies.

I know it was way more work than it would have been if we had just decorated with our family, but our parents really were the best when it came to creating an atmosphere of love, joy, chaos, and friendship.

Thanks for all of the awesome memories, Mom and Dad. It truly was the best night of the year.

MEDITATE OR MEDICATE

"If you think that you're enlightened,
go spend a week with your family."

—Ram Dass

For years, I was an aspiring meditator. I say aspiring because I spent more time considering it and talking about it than actually doing it.

I was a consistently inconsistent visitor to my meditation cushion. I was noncommittal. I was too busy. I was young. I was still coming to terms with just how much someone like me needed to have her butt glued to a meditation cushion.

When you find that you lose your center easily and lose your cool even faster, you deduce that either meditation or medication will be your salvation. But which is it?

Meditation being a regular practice was in some ways completely natural. I was already drawn to all things that smacked of self-reflection and calm. If ever there was a person who should've been a flower child it's me. In 1989, I was burning incense, candles and listening to Sarah McLachlan to the point it was possible I'd burn the house down or my mom would so she didn't have to listen to Sarah anymore. It was a toss up.

It was a departure to be cultivating quiet, being still, and contemplating a response when you come from a family that's loud, boisterous, and highly reactive. It's a large group with many personalities and widely varying opinions about everything except one thing: family first.

Family first over time morphs into involvement in everyone's day-to-day existence. You find you are kept up to date on your cousin's kid's cold, your aunt's latest bout with allergies, and whose spouse we are mad at today—out of familial solidarity, of course. We come from a serious group of worriers, perseverators, anticipators, and waiting for the other shoe to fall-ers. That quickly turns into a lot of mental chatter and more than a few triggers.

When our immediate family opted to celebrate a Colorado Christmas in July a few years ago, we had mostly everyone together. And as is the case, when you get your parents and siblings together, even when your driver's license claims you're an adult, everyone becomes 12 years old again. We fall into our old roles, our old habits, and before too long it feels like you're in the back of the minivan with no air conditioning on your way to Kings Island and you're sure your sister is touching you or looking at you or breathing on you.

One morning, Lowi and I headed out for an early hike and stopped at the top of a beautiful lookout over Lake Georgetown. It was quiet, peaceful, sunny, and a great chance to regroup. I didn't have any incense with me, but the thin air due to altitude was good enough. We stopped, each found a boulder to fill in as our meditation cushion, and meditated. I am not sure how long we were there and I don't think we said much to each other on the way back. We were able to sit and find our center again, even in our 12-year-old selves.

For me meditation became my Wonder Twin power because, frankly, no amount of medication can compete with family or your sister sitting too close to you.

LOWI
&
G

TEXTING WITH MOM AND DAD

"My mom says the apple doesn't fall far from the tree,
but I'm hopeful that their tree was on a hill
and I'm rolling farther away as I write."

—Kristin Billerbeck

Whenever we have the opportunity for some quality time with the parents they rarely disappoint in their ability to deliver some crazy antics.

Let's start with their ongoing alter egos that they've created for each other. For years our mom has referred to my dad and herself as Ward and June, respectively. It's a classic reference considering there isn't much about our parents that's 1950s.

Other times they've been temporarily referred to as Kim Kardashian and Kanye West after some ill-fated and misguided autocorrecting via text. Regardless, it's always a comedy of errors with these two and sometimes it leaves us questioning how we all made it out alive.

One afternoon the parental unit was stopping by for a visit. This can be a waiting game as my mom doesn't like to be kept to a schedule, especially if some sort of crisis might develop for which her services would be required. She always has errands to run, food to drop off at someone's house after their bunion surgery, or someone who needs checking on.

Add to that, as our parents age, they have decided that basic, direct routes anywhere are verboten. Once driving the highway was considered avant garde and chic. Now it's regarded much akin to mud on your shoe or the use of a navigation system. It's fallen out of favor. So you never know how long a 30-minute trip might take and what backwater, horse and buggy traveling, dirt-road path they might opt to take to my house. This only adds to the excitement. They could arrive in an hour, three, or next Tuesday.

Their relationship with technology is not much different. At times I wonder if they are thinking, "What is this fancy box that lights up?" That could be in reference to their cell phones, Kindle or TV.

Just the mere question of what the password is to their Wi-Fi access can take us down a tour of syntax, capitalization, and every pet name we can remember. It's an adventure.

One afternoon, after arriving by tractor from the back 40, Dad begins to regale us, first, with the story about when Mom was texting him, but thought she was texting her sister, Lisa.

The "Who's On First?" comedy routine commences with Mom continuing her line of commentary and questions about my aunt's meeting that day even though she's getting responses like this from my Dad:

What meeting?

What are you talking about?

and the best...

Is English your first language?

At this point, I am on the floor, squealing as I no longer have enough air for a proper laugh, tears are streaming, and my stomach hurts.

But the master of ceremonies, Big Papa Lou, was on a roll and he clearly was not done with texting stories. He continues to tell me that a few nights earlier he woke up to a strange sound. He opens his eyes and as he says, "I saw a bright light and thought 'I am crossing over!'"

Instead of crossing over, it was just Mom getting her full use of unlimited texting at 3:00 a.m. If not, I would have to say the cell reception in heaven is IM-PRESS-IVE!

Dad, without missing a beat, went to work the next day telling his co-workers he had a Near Death Experience!

Yep, texting with Mom and Dad is probably a lot like having coffee around the dinner table with Ward and June.

THE CANOE

"Up a creek without a paddle."

—Anonymous

There are some moments from childhood that bring fond memories even if at the time they weren't so pleasant. Like the time I got hit in the face with a baseball bat. Not so fun in the moment, but looking back at pictures with me sporting an impressive shiner are pretty entertaining.

And then there's the day Lowi and I went canoeing with our Dad and Grandpa. I was fairly young so I don't remember it exactly in chronological order, but more like snapshots. What I do remember is that the whole scenario was not engineered for little girls like Lowi and me.

We were moving along down the Little Darby Creek and I could almost taste the bug repellant OFF because it had been applied liberally and haphazardly by someone. I can still conjure up that feeling on my tongue.

Then a fish jumped into the canoe. I was losing it already. Fish, worms, slippery slimy things are not what little girls enjoy. At least it wasn't what I enjoyed.

My dad, however, remembers that I was quite concerned that the fish that recently joined our voyage was trying to eat my sister. Keep in mind I was likely under the age of 10 and anything is possible, right? What I know for sure is that I wanted to go home and that Mom was not going to be pleased about this fish situation.

Next thing I know we are in the water and Dad's wallet is floating along next to us but nice and dry in a Ziploc bag. Don't worry, we were wearing life jackets and before long Lowi and I were soaked but standing on the bank of the creek.

It's one of those childhood adventures that you don't really want to repeat.

But then decades later, our younger sister, Baby Lisa, and I got a text from Dad that went like this:

Dad

New life has been given to old canoe. Cleaned, licensed, and ready for shakedown cruise.

D

Baby Lisa

Nice!

BL

G

Oh my... I am having flashbacks of being drenched and standing on the shore all over again.

Dad

You will be able to relive those experiences over and over.

D

G

Yes, it's called PTSD.

Upon reflection I am still very sure I don't want to go canoeing.

PART 2

CHOOSE WISELY:

THIS WILL BE ON YOUR PERMANENT RECORD

"In the long run, we shape our lives, and we shape ourselves. The process never ends until we die. And the choices we make are ultimately our own responsibility."

—Eleanor Roosevelt

MARGARITAS? WE HAVE SALT!

"Why fit in when you were born to stand out?"

—Dr. Seuss

Part of self-reflection and self-evaluation is when your neighbors discover that you are a scosh weird. And just maybe, you realize it exactly at the same time.

You see, I'm one of the cat people. No this is not the thing that makes me weird. (OK, it's not the only thing.)

Anyway, one of my felines was hanging out at casa de vet and I was simultaneously experiencing a cash-ecto-my. I, however, was worried much less about the money and more about whether my furball was going to make it out with a few of his nine lives.

It was time to get serious. I did a fire ceremony on my front porch, I chanted, and I prayed. Then in an act of clearing energy and renewing the space, I was instructed to sprinkle kosher salt around my home.

OK, this wasn't my ceremony. If I remember correctly I found it on the internet, but desperate times and all.

I live in a condo, so if you are going to ring your home in salt you are in effect ringing three other families' homes, too. But really who can be bothered by freshened energy?

The next morning while outside, my neighbor was curiously looking at this ring of salt, but he didn't know what it was. Quickly into our morning pleasantries it becomes clear he's bothered—actually concerned—about the salt. (Maybe it's anthrax or some other deadly substance!)

Fearing he may call the EPA over kosher salt, I come clean about the energy and me.

So, as normally and briefly as possible I explain that I am responsible for the salt, that it's safe, and all is A-OK.

I won't say he backed away slowly or reached for his concealed weapon, but our conversation ended soon after.

But really, how bad is it that your neighbor ringed your home in kosher salt? It was kosher, and if you have margaritas later, you're set. We might have to extend the 5-second rule, but otherwise it's a win.

Later on I told my husband the story and he gave me a knowing laugh. He has learned, along with me, to embrace the totality of me. This life, it's a wild ride.

FILTERED SARCASM

"My natural-born sarcasm, when it's unimpeded, can be a bit overbearing at times and I'm the first to admit that."

—Tom Bergeron

My hubby wanted to know why I had to be so sarcastic.

I realize it's difficult to imagine, but it's true. Back in the day, my hubby didn't actually appreciate my sarcasm. In fact, there are still moments when he prefers I keep it under wraps.

When you grow up cutting your teeth on a survival skill like sarcasm it becomes second nature. It's not something you necessarily choose, it's just part of who you become. It's ingrained in the fabric of your being.

I know it sounds dramatic, but the first time my hubby expressed his disdain for my quick wit, it cut me to the core. In that moment, it became a character flaw that I had no idea how to fix. It felt like he was saying, "I would like you to be four inches taller, blonde, and have blue eyes." That was never going to happen, so I did what any sane person who was being attacked would do. I lashed out and explained (sarcastically, I might add) that like it or not he bought the whole package and guess what? Sarcasm was a main ingredient.

Inside I was reeling. How could the thing that helped me cling to the top of the heap in our family also be the flaw that made me not enough? The juxtaposition of these two things was maddening, and yet when I sat with it I realized he was kind of right. Logically, I knew he wasn't saying he didn't love me, that I wasn't kind, or that I couldn't be funny, he was asking me to use a filter.

Using a filter felt heavy, and it was exhausting.

I kept trying because we had children to raise and it turns out they aren't wired to understand sarcasm at an early age. They are literal beings and when you say things like, "No, it's OK. Just leave your toys all over the family room. I don't mind." They think you are serious and it's confusing to them when you are mad that they haven't cleaned up their toys. Kindness and clarity are much more helpful when raising young people.

In reality, my husband wasn't asking me to become someone different, he was just challenging me to be more of myself. What I discovered was that I, too, needed more than a healthy dose of sarcasm to get me through. I needed more sunshine.

I had a choice of how I wanted to be and who I wanted to be.

So, I began to open myself up to being more literal, more positive, and less snarky. When things didn't go quite as I had planned during a day of mothering I acknowledged that this is how life goes with small children. I didn't deflect my feelings of failure by making a snide comment. I just accepted it for what it was and that tomorrow was a new day. Some of these days it actually felt good to just be vulnerable about what my life looked like.

Then there were the days when it felt like the only thing to release the steam that was building inside of me was to cry, scream or get snarky. So, I did what anyone would do, I reverted back to my old habits. I cried and screamed at my husband that I couldn't be Mary Sunshine all the damn time! What can I say, everything is a process.

For me this process looked a lot like one step forward, three steps back. More specifically it looked like lots of prayer, pain, illness, love, failure, joy, laughter, meditation, patience, running, journaling, reading, and...lots of humor. This is also around the same time that I began to find solace in not just running, but testing my limits. If I could run five miles I wanted to know if I could run 10. I didn't care about the speed as much as how far I could go. I think it was my subconscious taking a deep breath and showing me I could move in a different direction. What I have learned along the way is that if we allow ourselves to open up to the possibility that we can be more...we can.

Author's note: My three girls are patient, kind, wise, and they all have a wicked sense of humor.

DUMB IT DOWN?

*"Maybe our girlfriends are our soulmates and
guys are just people to have fun with."*

—Candace Bushnell

M y middle daughter, Sydney, is a spark plug. She has
a huge personality and enough energy for five people. She is passionate about everything she does and
for the most part, she is fearless.

She is also very bright.

On her 14th birthday we were celebrating with gifts,
pizza, and laughter. A story came to light about Sydney skiing with a certain boy on her team... alone. Jokes
were made, the story was partially refuted and then her
older sister, Alex, wanted to know how she did it. Alex
demanded to know how Sydney seemed to always have
a boy chasing her when she was unable to get a boy to

"WHAT CAN I SAY, MIND READING IS STILL NOT THEIR FORTÉ."

even look at her. Sydney looked at her and very seriously said, "You gotta dumb it down a little, Alex."

Alex was indignant and said she wouldn't dumb it down for anyone. Amen, sister!

Over the next week we had a lot of laughs about this conversation, but I was curious what Sydney was really thinking when she said, "You gotta dumb it down." Did she really think that boys like dumb girls or does she think all boys were dumb?

It turned out that she didn't believe either of these things. She said she knew she was smart and she believed people thought that of her as well. In all her 14-year-old wisdom she said, "Boys just like you to be silly with them. They don't like it when we act like they are disgusting or immature. They don't want to participate in girl drama and they definitely don't like it when we are mysterious. They have a hard enough time figuring us out. They just want us to be real and accept them for who they are. Just like we want to be accepted for who we are. So, when I say that I "dumb it down" I mean I am just being who I am, having fun, and being one of the guys."

Apparently, I didn't have to be worried about Sydney playing dumb. She had it under control. My only advice to Sydney was, "Don't dumb it down too much, baby!"

I asked Sydney how she felt about these words of wisdom five years later. She responded, "Wow! Those are some wise words from my 14-year-old self! While I don't know if I would necessarily use the words 'dumbing it down' today, I do believe the message is still valid. At 19, I believe that guys want to be with someone who is intelligent, enjoys their company, accepts them for who they are without trying to change them, is confident in who they are, doesn't create drama that requires damage control every other Tuesday night, and is straight up about who they are and what they want. What can I say, mind reading is still not their forté."

PAIN LEARNER /JOY LEARNER

"There is no hurry anywhere else except in your mind. If you really want to be in a state of peace and joy, you will have to unlearn your old habit for achieving things quickly, fast."

—Ritu Ghatourey

Unconsciously, I always knew I was a pain learner. By pain, I do not necessarily mean physical pain, but I needed a real jolt to get me going. Stub your toe while walking barefoot— learn to start wearing shoes. Crash and burn during a work presentation—learn to go through it with a coworker beforehand.

It never occurred to me that I could learn through joy, or maybe, I just never expected joy to be a good teacher.

I went to a yoga workshop the weekend after accomplishing a long-time goal of running, walking, and stumbling through 50 miles. Not too far into the day,

Judith Hanson Lasater nearly pushed me to a full-on cry. She did bring the tears, they just wouldn't spill. I wouldn't let them.

Lasater suggested we humans are good at learning from pain and I could feel the tears begin to well up. Not only had I learned from pain, I had often created "painful" situations to spur growth. I set up benchmarks that required some level of spiritual, emotional or physical bloodshed to grow.

The idea that learning through joy was even an option kinda blew my mind. I'd just spent the last six months training to be able to cover 50 miles, in one day, by foot. A goal I wanted to reach desperately, but I often doubted my ability and my mental toughness. I doubted if I could, or would, or was willing to suffer that much. I've learned a lot by running ultra distances, but my doubts, insecurities, and anxiety about it have also plagued me.

A continuous crisis of confidence.

On the heels of having accomplished the goal and, looking back now, still being pretty raw emotionally and physically, I went to the workshop open. I didn't have the energy to be closed.

If I could hit the 50-mile mark, I would find confidence. If I could keep moving for 16 hours I would become more mentally tough. If I could run 22 miles into the night, on a treadmill, in the dark, I would be good enough, OK enough ... for what?

These are big tells.

It's not an accident that I began saying I run ultra distances instead of I am an ultrarunner. I don't feel worthy of saying I am an ultrarunner. I am too slow, too fearful. I really think I run distances that are too short. I take walk breaks. I have a million reasons why I am not good enough.

All of them lead back to being a pain learner or thinking I need to be.

This one I was willing to take in. I am ready to find—know—a better way.

I want to learn from happiness. I don't want to be a foreboder of joy. I don't want to be waiting for the other shoe to fall to make the matching set of gloom and doom.

Can I learn from being happy? I don't know, but maybe that is only because I never tried.

I COULD BE AWESOME-ISH!

"One of the hardest parts of life is deciding whether to walk away or try harder."

—Anonymous

've never been much of an overachiever in life. I am middle of the road. I am what you'd call basic. But, I have big dreams and I want to live a big life.

I mean, Lowi and I have a blog and we're proud of the work we do the majority of the time. But when your Mom, Dad, and a smattering of friends read it most days you're not quite a rousing success.

If you are reading this book, you are likely among the number of purchasers we can count on one hand and still have a few digits leftover for wild or obscene gesturing if the situation warranted it.

Wanting to live an epic life doesn't necessarily translate into fame or adulation.

I don't excel in any arena except maybe being dramatic and being able to tie a cherry stem in a knot in my mouth. Neither of which are terribly marketable skills if you aren't an actor and you don't want to work in the red light district.

I've never entered anything with the thought of winning. I'm a small town girl and while I've grown up and moved on, I still see myself much that way. When someone asks me what I am good at it's usually something I have to think about for a while. And then I say, well ... I don't know. Let me think some more.

It's tough to think about what you are good at because most of us are still trying to figure out who we are. Finding clarity about who you are can be complicated. You need to get clear in your own head and not let the input of others muddy that water. It's like for the first several decades of your life you're in one very long eye exam. Your vision is blurred and your pupils are dilated. You have to be driven around by your mom and you have these big, bulky dark sunglasses on that make it impossible to see anything clearly.

You never know how to see yourself and through whose lenses you are looking. I think by the time you're awarded your AARP card and bifocals you finally start to figure it all out—a little. But, early on we get all our information filtered through others.

"You're a little princess."

"You're a big boy"

"You're a tough kiddo."

You're a _____. (The blank is always filled in by someone else.)

Finally into my fourth decade, I'm realizing that this onion is taking a tad longer to peel than anticipated. And there will be tears, guaranteed.

It's because we're unprepared. We often confuse what we do with who we are and those really are two different concepts. They take time to work through if you ever thoroughly get it straight at all.

So like I said, I need time to think about my talents.

I can spell, some would say I often use Scrabble-worthy vocabulary, and I can string words together without too much head bashing. I can cook. I can bake. If really backed into a corner, I would say I have had moments of being awesome-ish.

Is that something like being Amish with a few extra letters? Probably not since I can't even sew a button back on, and I don't really know how to work with horses. I identify more with the -ish.

I am smart-ish, kind-ish, mostly fun-ish...

DREAM-FOLLOWING IS SUCCESS

"Your time is too valuable to be distracted by negative people. Don't let anyone talk you out of your dreams."

—Joel Osteen

For some reason, we only love dream followers in theory. We're only "all for it" after we know how it works out in the end. When it's still to be determined or it turns out another way, we call it foolish. We call it failure.

But is it? Is living on peanut butter sandwiches for a year to pursue what you love any less brave or amazing if it doesn't work out? Is it only cool and avant-garde to live in your car for your art if later you're a millionaire painter?

If you really, honestly—without judgment—think about it, the first step IS success.

You've decided to swim upstream.

You've decided to go where your heart tells you.

You've decided to be guided by love.

You've decided to go against a constant barrage of critique, commentary, and naysayers.

*You're doing, if we're brutally honest about it, what the rest of us are **too damn scared to do**.*

*In fact, it's so true that I will say it again: The rest of us are **TOO SCARED!***

But that fear often manifests into judgment because subconsciously it makes us feel better. It soothes our own too tender egos and helps us to forget our own uncharted paths that have collected dust. That's painful, so often we lash out a little too quickly, a little too dismissively, with flip comments.

I have done it many a time and it's not something that makes me proud. But as I get older, and hopefully a wee bit wiser, I am learning to recognize when someone's striving has hit my fear nerve.

It's hit the vulnerable spot in me that knows they are doing something I was or am far too afraid to do: Try.

So what do we do? Let's start by doing more things that scare us. Let's do more things that make our mouths run dry and our pulses race.

Let's DO!

And the next time you hear about someone running off on what seems to you like a crazy path, ask yourself: Who's talking? Your Fear? Or your bravery?

PLAN B?

*"Faith is taking the first step even when
you don't see the whole staircase."*

—Martin Luther King, Jr.

I had a conversation with a close family friend in which she was voicing her concern for my adult children. It's important for you to understand that this concern was centered around my two oldest daughters who were beginning new chapters in their lives. To be clear, I worry about both of them every single day. I pray that they are making wise decisions and that they will only cross paths with those who have their best interest at heart, but I am not about to let anyone see me sweat.

They are both in the business of hunting down dreams, breaking down walls, and stomping out fear. Parental stress inherently comes with the territory.

My friend wasn't pleased with what seemed like my nonchalant attitude in the midst of her "very real concern" over my children. She told me she would just have to get used to my girls' free-spirited approach because that is the way I raised them.

This friend is awesome and supportive, but this did not feel like a compliment, I can assure you. It didn't feel like she was saying that she knew they would be fine because I had done such a great job as a mother. It felt more like, "What the $*%$@ is wrong with you letting your girls just go chase after their dreams without some kind of plan to catch them when they fall?" Now, I know this is just her fear speaking and she really is proud of them. Doing real life is scary sometimes. I get it.

And I have a plan. It's called faith. Faith that no matter what happens, we will deal with it; faith that God did not bring them this far to drop them on their pretty little heads. And yes, I am scared out of my mind some days, but I would not want for anything less. Why? Because I did raise them to be smart, strong, independent, crazy dreamers who can do anything they want if they work hard enough for it. Their dream might end up looking radically different than when they began. They might take a detour or two. They might fail miserably. That's OK, because none of us knows what lies on the path ahead...until we begin.

TRANSITION

*"Do not go where the path may lead; go instead
where there is no path and leave a trail."*

—Ralph Waldo Emerson

Saying goodbye to one of your children when you know months will pass before you see them again causes mixed feelings. I have done this before and survived. We took our oldest to college two years ago and that was a difficult goodbye. Not because she was far away, but because it's a milestone moment. It marks a time when things begin to change. Our kids are not little anymore. Yes, they still ask for advice and in most cases are still receiving financial support, but it's never the same after they've moved out. In fact, I am pretty sure our oldest prefers to be in Boulder with her friends and in her apartment over being with the family. That is what is supposed to happen and I believe the mark by which we measure if we have done our job. We want them to be strong and independent adults. Right?

While we were on a vacation, I watched our three daughters paddle board and swim in the ocean together. It was bittersweet because I kept thinking this might be the last time we get to do this as a family. Sure, we might all vacation together again, but the dynamics will be different. I was choked up thinking about it and envisioning them as little girls at the beach, building sand castles, and trying to knock one another off the boogie board.

When we returned from vacation, I prepared to say goodbye to our middle daughter and our oldest within the same week. As I left my middle one in Nashville, I prepped myself for the onslaught of emotions. Had I taught her everything she needed to know to live on her own? Had I reminded her at least 20 times of the really important things: her morals and values, safety, and boys? I'd wanted to stay and make sure she had a job, a church, a schedule, a group of friends, and so much more. As I drove away though, I realized that while she was young, independent, and stubborn she also believed she could do anything—and she can.

At that same moment I was sending my oldest daughter off into the world. She was going on a medical mission to work with mamas and babies in Haiti. She could not wait and her heart was full of joy, hope, and a spirit that was contagious. I could not have been more proud of her. This was something she had been wanting to do for years and it was finally coming to fruition. I knew she would be blessed immensely by this experience, but I also knew she would be a tremendous blessing as well.

I knew at the time and now that there were bigger things happening in the world and many of you have faced much larger challenges, but sending two of my girls off in a week's time was hard. I have a friend who was in a similar situation with her kids going off to be adults like we raised them to be, and when I asked her how she was feeling she said,

"MY HEART IS FULL AND HEAVY AT THE SAME TIME."

What an absolutely perfect way to describe this time in our lives.

Now, don't get me wrong, this is all wonderful. I am a proud mama and I want my girls to go conquer the world...theoretically. I guess I am just wondering why they can't conquer the world right here in our county? I know all the mamas out there who have sent their children off into the world (including ours) have survived and even thrived, but my heart is a little tender right now. I also know that there are mamas out there sending their babies off to preschool and kindergarten, and they are shedding some tears as well.

My advice to them?

Hold them tight, love them with everything you have, and be present for every moment.

THE NATURE OF WONDER

*"A strong friendship doesn't need daily conversation;
doesn't always need togetherness. As long as the relationship
lives in the heart, true friends will never part."*

—Anonymous

I have become a novice gardener in the last few years. We started out with a few herbs and each year we've slowly added on, learned more, and gotten better. Regardless of how much we know, or think we know, one thing remains true: no matter how much love and attention and "food" you give the plants, some will thrive due to your efforts and others will wither in spite of them. It seems the nature of things.

Relationships aren't much different. We've all had couplings that didn't work out, friendships that fizzled, and other co-minglings that imploded. And into some of those pairings we put time, energy, love, compromise, and genuine effort into helping them succeed and they just didn't.

Meanwhile, others flourish and expand despite the fact that you've left them out in the beating sun, not protected them from frost, and let the weeds grow up around the roots for weeks, months or years. Those connections, for whatever reason, are hardy; seemingly unbreakable.

Why is that? Some people or connections we care for like fragile angel wings. We guard them, shower them with love, and yet disintegration begins almost from the outset. While others we tend to much like our gym bag. It gets thrown in the trunk, dropped at our feet, and sometimes overlooked for months.

I'm not sure if there is an answer here, but I am sure that if there is, I don't know it yet. Maybe it's the magic of our interconnectedness. The quirky-ness of how life works out or doesn't.

I had lunch with a wonderful friend and while we've been buddies for more than a decade, ours is an untended garden. There are more than enough weeds and neglect to have long since strangled its joy and yet it continues on, uninterrupted by time, space or lack of consistent watering or feeding. It's the inexplicable quality that makes life an entity that can only be experienced.

Sometimes "why" doesn't matter. Maybe welcoming the incongruities and unmatched pieces of life is all part of the wonder.

SOMETIMES WHY DOESN'T MATTER

DO HARD THINGS

*"It's OK to be scared. Being scared means you're
about to do something really, really brave."*

—Mandy Hale

D o more of the things that leave you feeling blissful in its residue. Do more things that make you happy just for the doing. Strangely, sometimes those things are also the most challenging ones.

Do Hard Things!

It's a simple motto that we've all heard. It's a life metaphor, or directive, that's worthwhile and never stops being good advice. Doing something that stretches you or pushes you makes the accomplishment sweeter, the getting there... more, well, MORE. It builds the appetite for striving.

It's stoking the fire of always moving forward. Moving, not because we'd rather be anywhere but here, but in the service of showing up in this life.

It's about the term used by Mihaly Csikszentmihalyi in "Flow" known as *optimal experience... a sense of exhilaration, a deep sense of enjoyment that is long cherished and that becomes a landmark in memory for what life should be like.*"

"*The best moments in our lives, are not the passive, receptive, relaxing times —although such experiences can also be enjoyable, if we have worked hard to attain them. The best moments usually occur when a person's body or mind is stretched to its limits in a voluntary effort to accomplish something difficult and worthwhile. Optimal experience is thus something that we make happen...that comes as close to what is usually meant by happiness as anything else we can conceivably imagine.*"

What are we doing to expand our limits? What are we working hard to attain?

Life is meant to be full of experiences, uncontrollable forces, and amazing smiles. All of that comes from getting out of our routine, our comfort zone or expertise, and opening arms wide to life.

Are you open?

TRIBE-WORTHY

"Surround yourself with the dreamers and the doers, the believers and thinkers, but most of all, surround yourself with those who see greatness within you, even when you don't see it yourself."

—Edmund Lee

I have had some great learning experiences and as the late, great Maya Angelou cautioned, when people show you who they are, you should believe them. Similarly so, when it seems like someone doesn't value you, your time, or your contribution—they don't. So stop already.

All it really means is you are not in their tribe, they are not in yours. It doesn't mean war—just stop forcing it and accept.

Some relationships, moments, and connections are simple from the beginning. They click (not to be confused with clique).

And others (and you know it almost immediately whether you admit it or not) are forced. You make excuses, you bend yourself a little, you box yourself up a little more, trying to make it work. As Brené Brown, our guru, would say, you're hustling for worthiness.

Thankfully, and I do mean this sincerely, I had these two kinds of opposing experiences in a short span of time. And that juxtaposition was needed. These experiences butted up against one another. They collided in my brain when I thought about them. Their mismatched edges were unmistakable as was how I felt about them.

♕ FEELING WORTHY. HUSTLING TO FEEL WORTHY.

Any way you dress it up, that's what it is. Some relationships and interactions allow me to feel instantly like I am part of their group, and further, I know I want these people to be part of mine. We are in the same tribe.

And others leave you feeling more like you need triage. You walk away feeling emotionally worn from trying to push and twist your way into this belonging that feels unnatural.

I am getting too old to hustle, to not feel worthy, and to be making excuses. Aren't we all?

We don't like everyone, we're likely not supposed to. Everyone doesn't like us, they're likely not supposed to (that's a tough pill, I know). But let's be honest with ourselves about it. Next time you walk away from a social experience, ask yourself: "Did I feel tribe-worthy or triage-needing?"

When you get the answer, trust it!

THE BEGINNING OF BALANCE

"Real change isn't found in some new way to think about yourself, but in freedom from the need to think about yourself at all."

—Guy Finley

I had a career—a byline—I had an education. I even had a husband.

Shock of it all? I walked away from three of the four.

I still have the husband, but at 27 I decided to change my career. I went back to school part time and slowly began to change my life.

I think that's where the sunshine started to peek in through the sarcasm clouds.

Like the rest of my life, not much is linear. After you earn a bachelor's degree it's only natural to go to your local community college for an associate's degree. (There's that sarcasm I was referring to...)

After years of part-time dead-end jobs as a teenager and college student, I was now the most overqualified receptionist/salesperson ever. OK, maybe not ever, but still...

And I was negative. At the time, I probably wouldn't have categorized myself as unhappy or surly, but I was.

When I say I was unhappy, I was really a malcontent. I was always seeing the glass half empty, always complaining. Don't get me wrong, I am still in a 12-step program for the discontented, so if you are thinking... Hmm I think I still see those qualities in her... You'd be right. But I am better today than yesterday and so on.

Around my mid 30s I found myself in what you might call a dark night of the soul. An inexplicable loss of a friendship and the subsequent loss of faith in my basic goodness as a human being, sent me circling the drain.

It was a rough time and a real transition point. My sarcasm was not going to save me. I realized I didn't have another way to deal with what I was experiencing at the ready.

I began really seeking. I was open to try anything because I was in such a low place. The searcher in me was born. Before I was a dabbler, an experimenter, because it was fun. However, now my seeking was becoming more of a necessity to get through the day.

Seeing only the wrong of life wasn't getting me out of bed.

Noticing only the incongruities, while possibly amusing, wasn't making me feel better about myself.

I started reading—a lot.

I started to find teachers that resonated with me in a way that I needed.

- Debbie Ford

- Marianne Williamson

- Louise Hay

- Cheryl Richardson

- Byron Katie

- Elizabeth Gilbert

- Gabrielle Bernstein

- Melody Beattie

- Rick Hanson

- Brené Brown

- Elizabeth Lesser

Plus many more I am not remembering in this moment.

I found that I didn't have a meaningful life process to guide me through. I didn't have a faith, a religion that spoke to who I was in that moment. I started examining the way those around me operated. That left me wanting as well. Fear was the prevailing mode of existence, and I knew praying at the altar of fear wasn't going to be useful to me. I was in a tough spot, and I needed help. For the first time sarcasm wasn't going to be my guiding light, and I didn't have another skill set.

Slowly I began cobbling together a new way of being. I started taking my personal yoga practice more seriously. I started participating in a style of spirituality that made sense for me and I got professional help. It was time. Slower than I ever imagined, I started to regain faith in myself again. That while I was flawed, mistake-ridden, and confused, I was still OK. I could still move forward.

I started to practice gratitude. With time I started to feel it as well.

My meditation practice became more consistent, more meaningful, and it gave me more of myself back.

The sun began to emerge.

This was the true beginning of my complicated but rewarding relationship between sunshine and sarcasm in my life. At that moment, the teeter-totter of sunshine and sarcasm began to tip back and forth and sometimes holds its near-impossible balance in the middle.

CAT LADY

"Every girl is a crazy cat lady. If she says she is not then it is your duty to assure her that she is indeed a crazy cat lady."

—Unknown

In life there appears to be a preferred order to things, and you barely accomplish one of the to-dos on the list and then you're being asked about the next one. Two things have become quite clear:

1. NOBODY LIKES IT WHEN YOU DO THINGS OUT OF ORDER.

2. NOBODY LIKES IT WHEN YOU SKIP STEPS.

You can see where this is going... Nobody is happy!

Not long after my husband and I got married, the talk of children quickly and deafeningly began. It's important to note before we go any further because people often misunderstand or misinterpret... I like kids and I love my nieces. But I think the decision to parent should involve a bit more thought than, wow—tab B fits into slot A equals baby.

I figured out early on that being a mom was not my jam. And nobody was happy.

But when John and I decided to expand our family in an alternate way, I didn't anticipate how it would change others' perception of me.

Growing up we had a menagerie of animals over the years from hamsters to goldfish, cats and dogs. My husband was, however, paws down a cat person.

We went to the nearby shelter to adopt our first feline delight. We eventually decided on Basil, he already had that name and it seemed perfect.

Quickly, we realized he was perfectly sick.

After several days in an incubator and a large cash donation to the local vet, Basil came home with a clean bill of health. With some good healing, we realized what a hellion he actually was.

After much chachki breaking, Christmas tree jumping, pant leg climbing and aerial flying from the stairwell.... We decided, of course, we needed another cat.

OK, we didn't decide. Instead, I got sucked in by a shelter cat at PetsMart. It only took one week of whining to have John give in. And then, another large vet donation later, our meow-less, eye-infected, ear mite-infested cat came home. Her shelter name was Holly and we weren't feeling the festive spirit so she instead became known as Parsley.

So that's my family of four. I treat my animals like they are my kids as most anyone who knows me would attest to. It's particularly awkward when someone asks if I have children and other friends or family jump in to say, "She has cats!"

It's much like saying, she has dementia. She has some sort of brain-eating amoeba.

It draws a horrified look that's dashed with a glancing blow of sympathy and then a heavy dollop of judgment. Nobody is happy.

Then after you spend a few painful minutes frantically trying to talk it down, tone it down you realize the cat is out of the bag and meowing loudly. You are now and forever after a crazy cat lady in their eyes.

My life is out of order, I skipped steps, and I am still happy.

HOME IS WHERE THE CAT IS

PART 3

NOT WHAT
I WAS
EXPECTING

"Most people want to be circled by safety, not by the unexpected. The unexpected can take you out. But the unexpected can also take you over and change your life. Put a heart in your body where a stone used to be."

— Ron Hall

BEST TIMES ARE AWAITING US

*"What a wonderful thought it is that some of the
best days of our lives haven't happened yet."*

—Quotebites.com

We go through stages of nostalgia remembering good times and events past, and it's easy to get caught up in the idea that all the "bests" of life have somehow passed along with our youth. But that's far from true.

Think of all the amazing and fulfilling things that happen to us later in our lives. Many of us will, or have, become grandparents long after we are in our 40s. Even our mid-life crises make us better on the far side. At a certain point, we begin to learn that we can't do it all and usually don't even want to and with that comes freedom. Joy usually quickly follows that. And I am hoping wisdom quickly trails in on joy's heels.

For me, I certainly don't want to look back and think that my high school or college days were the best of my life. I don't believe it's true. While there were plenty of good memories, I would feel incredibly empty to think that's it.

In the last few years, I have had the opportunity to experience amazing highs that I never would've dreamed of or even been interested in when I was 20-something. Those moments would've been wasted on my younger self.

I wouldn't have been able to appreciate being in stillness and quiet with another, but sometimes that's enough.

I couldn't have fully grasped the joy in watching my nieces graduate high school and further seeing them follow big dreams with more bravery than fear.

Since college, I have learned the difference between enjoying the fun parts of family and embracing the fullness of having a place you always belong.

Awe-inspiring, jaw-dropping, tear-inducing days, glimpses, and years are still awaiting you and me.

I AM SMARTER THAN YOU:
I AM FLUENT IN SARCASM

*"I'm not sarcastic. I'm just intelligent
beyond your understanding."*

—CoolnSmart.com

Some people might say that sarcasm is a curse. I, on the other hand, consider it a gift even though my husband has gently suggested a time or two that it's something I could possibly temper. I have always felt that was like asking someone to stop speaking their native language just because you couldn't speak it. I mean, I felt sorry for him and wished there was a Rosetta Stone for Sarcasm so he could work on it in his spare time, but this doesn't seem to be available as far as language options go.

I also had a difficult time keeping the sarcasm to a minimum when out in public. When you are fluent in a language it is challenging to keep it from just spewing out in the middle of a dinner party or even at the grocery store. It's especially humiliating when your native tongue slips out of your mouth and is met by blank stares. I often felt that I was less than because I didn't speak the same language as some of these other people.

And then I read an article that changed my life. OK, maybe it didn't change my life, but it sure did make for a satisfying conversation with my hubby and G! I had spent 20-some years trying to put a filter on my sarcasm because someone might find it offensive, and now I had proof that maybe they just felt threatened by my intelligence.

A study published in *Smithsonian Magazine* found that sarcastic people (Lowi & G) "have been found to be scientifically smarter." Richard Chin goes on to say, **"sarcasm requires a series of 'mental gymnastics.'** Sarcastic, satirical or ironic statements all compel the brain to 'think beyond the literal meaning of the words and understand that the speaker may be thinking of something entirely different.'"

Dan Scotti from Elite Daily covered this story and explained that, "in a way, sarcasm forces us to think one step ahead—a notion that science defends. In one experiment, by attaching electrodes to the brain and monitoring their activity (in response to sarcastic and non-sarcastic statements), electrical activity levels were increased when test subjects were exposed to sarcasm."

So, G and I will just be sitting over here doing our mental gymnastics in our own personal talented and gifted program. We will try not to look down on you if sarcasm is difficult for you to understand. We realize not everyone has been gifted with an intelligence like ours.

YOU CAN CALL ME LAKSHMI

"I don't believe an accident of birth makes people
sisters or brothers. It makes them siblings, gives them
mutuality of parentage. Sisterhood and brotherhood
is a condition people have to work at."

—Maya Angelou

I have an affinity for making fast friends. On a flight from Nashville to Newark I was unofficially adopted by an Indian woman.

First of all, because I changed my flight and was trying not to spend a fortune to get home, I bought a ticket from Nashville to Denver with a stop in Newark, New Jersey. Not exactly a direct flight, but hey, I had never been to New Jersey so now I can mark that off of my bucket list.

Anyway, just before the plane shut its doors a little Indian woman boarded. With plenty of open seats, it never occurred to me that she would want to sit between me and the narcoleptic by the window, but alas she felt my energy and could not resist. When she stopped at my row and looked at me I—literally—felt like I had somehow been "chosen."

She proceeded to sit down with her beautiful sari and peaceful aura, and with one look in my direction I knew it was going to happen: we were going to be fast friends.

I began by admiring her sari and mentioned that we have several at home that my hubby has brought back from his many trips to India. There was a little small talk and then the iPad came out. Soon she was showing me photos of her three grown sons, their wives, her grandchildren, and her friends. I have seen photos of graduation, prom, and each of their beautiful homes. Two of her sons live in the U.S. and one lives in India, and what a beautiful family. In fact, she was traveling to New Jersey to stay with one of her sons through the holidays.

Of course, she wanted to see photos of my family and hear about what each of my girls were like. Next thing I know, she asks me to take a selfie with her. We each took photos and then she took it one step further and asked me to email her. Because her English was pretty broken and because I was practically in her lap straining to hear her already, I asked her to type her email into my phone for me.

Suffice it to say, we continued our conversation throughout the flight and by the time we arrived in Newark she was holding my hand and telling me I was the daughter she never had. At this point, our narcoleptic neighbor had emerged from her slumber and, clearly, thought she had entered the twilight zone from the look on her face. Obviously, she doesn't know how to make fast friends.

I have been instructed to visit my newly adopted mother, Lalitha, in India and she has promised to cook for me and take me to the Taj Mahal. I can't even begin to tell you how amazing this woman was, but I think the email I received from her son a couple of days later might help you to understand. As an added bonus, I have a brother in New Jersey! I always wanted a brother.

> *Hi Lori:*
>
> *This is Raj. I am writing on behalf of my mom since she is not familiar with sending out emails yet. We are working on it. She was thrilled after she saw your email.*
>
> *When I picked her up from the airport the first thing she said to me was, "I now have*

a daughter in Denver." We know all about you and your three girls.

Please stay in touch and if you get a chance send my mom a picture of your family. If you are ever in the Tri-state area let us know.

Raj

People, we need to be open to what the universe has to offer. There are a lot of brothers and sisters out there just waiting to connect with us. Oh, and from now on you can call me by my Indian name, Lakshmi!

JOY AND WOE

"Man was made for joy and woe; And when this we rightly know. Through the world we safely go. Joy and woe are woven fine, A clothing for the soul divine."

—William Blake

Recently, I—along with several others—visited a friend who is ill. It was a bittersweet trip as her prognosis looks bleak. As we gathered outside on her plantation-style wraparound porch a fine rain fell to the ground. There was a sense of hush and quiet that was only intensified by the rain. Cool spring air and dampness instinctively urge you to draw near to each other and this kind of weather creates a closeness that the sun often burns off.

We sat around in rocking chairs and swings sharing stories of our own and a collection of others' letters of love and appreciation.

But more than that, we shared silence. We shared a communal space to hear the birds, the rain, the trees as they bent to and fro in the soft breeze. We heard the plodding footfalls of nearby cows, and we were present. The silence was heavy with sadness and what we feared for the future. And it was electric with the group's energy and desire to hold this kind of space.

Tears were shed often and freely as were smiles and laughter. During this experience, one person shared reading a book on the flight the day before. And a quote by William Blake caught her attention:

"JOY AND WOE ARE WOVEN FINE."

They are and they were on that Saturday afternoon. I never knew how close until then.

Not long after we shared this time together on the porch, it was time to head for home. With heaviness and almost a sense of finality we departed the long, wet gravel drive. I could see the gorgeous, southern, pillared home in the rearview mirror. But when I looked ahead I am carrying it all with me.

LOVE IS A CHOICE

*"I accept him, I love him, just as he is. He accepts me,
loves me, just as I am. We choose each other. Everyday.
It isn't puppies and rainbows and cotton candy under a
starry sky. But it's the biggest love that I've ever known."*

—Ritu Ghatourey

was listening to a song on the radio about falling in love. The song leaves you believing that when it comes to love you have no choice, but I believe every day we wake up and we choose who and what we are going to love.

While it's true that sometimes love comes walking in our door when we aren't looking for it and he or she looks completely different than we would have expected, we still have to choose whether to love this person.

Let's face it, once the crazy, I can't stand to be away from you, I can't keep my hands to myself phase has subsided you begin to see that he has just as many imperfections as you. OK, maybe he has more, but you know what I mean. You have to make a choice whether to accept this person, flaws and all, or move on.

When you are young and in love you can't imagine that someday long after the wedding and maybe kids that you will look at that person and think, "I am not sure I even like you." It's true and it's going to happen. But you committed to this person and this relationship and deep, deep down you know you chose to love this person. And if you are honest you know he is having to dig much deeper to choose loving you right now.

Since I have three girls I sometimes worry that the generation of young people who are in relationships today believe that love is like a romantic comedy. Love is not about candy, flowers, and big romantic gestures (although these things are always appreciated). Of course, we all want to laugh, have our hand held, and live happily ever after. Choosing to love someone though is holding her head out of the toilet when she is sick, taking the baby when he knows you have been up all night, making dinner when you just want to crawl in bed, rubbing HIS back when YOU hurt all over, and standing beside one another when your child is sick and hurting. Choosing to love is what will get you through, not flowers.

Life is not always smooth sailing and if you have been married long enough you know that there will be lots of love, joy, and laughter, but there will be equal parts illness, despair, and just plain tough times.

Real life happens every day and when you are faced with difficult times you want to be sure that the person standing next to you is someone you chose to be with, not just someone who walked in at the right time.

Be intentional in who you choose to love. Be intentional in the giving of that love.

Like our mom used to say, "make good choices."

"CHOOSING TO LOVE IS WHAT WILL GET YOU THROUGH, NOT FLOWERS."

SACRED

"When you try to control everything, you enjoy nothing. Relax, breathe, let go, and just live."

—Unknown

I began percolating on the idea of creating a yearly theme since G told me about hers a while back.

G even let me share in her EPIC theme by training and running a 50-mile ultra. She is such a giver. However, just because G began creating annual themes did not mean I was going to do it. I wanted to ponder it for awhile. I am one of those people that sometimes has to sit with something for a very long time before I actually take action.

It turns out that it would be a journey of the mind and soul for me.

When I sat down to think about how I wanted my new year to be, I thought a lot about certain moments from the previous year. The reason for this was not because I wanted to go back, but rather I wanted to remember the moments where I felt I was at my best. What was I doing? What did it feel like? How did I get there? Who was I in that moment? These are some of the questions I asked myself as I sat down to write out my goals for this year.

What I realized is that I had some great moments and I wanted more of them in this bright, shiny New Year. I also realized that how I wanted to feel during the year was absolutely the key to creating my goals and wrapping a theme around them. I wanted my year to be Epic, Boundless, Awesome, and Big like G's, but I just couldn't get there. While we have a tendency to share a brain a lot, this wasn't one of those times. Our lives are completely different and when it comes to creating goals and themes I needed to understand that while we might share some of the same goals, our journey to achieving them might look totally different.

So, I put G out of my head and started thinking about what I really wanted to accomplish.

What was I feeling during those moments that really mattered? I was feeling MORE. I was feeling WHOLE. I was in a SACRED SPACE.

THAT WAS IT! SACRED!

I know, it sounds like my goal was to sit in church the entire year and while I perhaps needed to sit in church for a solid year, that was not my intent.

I wanted my year to have value and I wanted to respect it. I wanted reaching my goals to feel like a religious experience. I wanted to feel connected to God and to what was around me. I wanted my family, my home, the things in it, my friends, my training, my routine to all be sacred to me. Maybe you are reading this right now and you have no idea what I am talking about and that's OK because, it only had to mean something to me.

So how did it go? Well, a lot of us make resolutions in the new year that never come to fruition. Sure, on January 1st we have the best of intentions, but something called life intervenes and then anything can happen. This year, my life felt a little like people had carjacked me and then asked me to stay and drive them wherever they might want to go.

When I began my year of being intentionally sacred, I had goals and expectations. Pretty quickly, like two days in, I realized that things were already taking a turn. I wouldn't say for the bad, but compromises were already being made. Trainings for my races were being postponed and eventually tossed out the window. My business took a back burner and even time with friends grew less and less. By mid-February I was getting frustrated and vowed to not cancel my races. I WOULD have a sacred year, damn it!

Life continued to throw curve balls and even holidays like Easter that are by nature sacred, were threatened by the chaos. And then it happened. I had to back out of a big race I had done the previous year with G. It felt like I was failing miserably at this sacred thing and I wondered if I could still salvage the pieces and turn this year around.

Six months into my year I chose to run a half marathon because I had already bailed out of one race and I surely couldn't look at myself in the mirror if I backed out of a measly 13.1 miles, right? Well, as it turns out I couldn't look at myself in the mirror because I could barely stand up after that half! Who was I kidding? I am not 25 anymore and I can no longer just go run a half marathon on the merits of my "running base." That and I had no base...because news flash, I wasn't actually training. Turns out that training actually is the best predictor of doing any kind of race well. Also, note to self: plowing through 13.1 miles because you said you would DOES NOT FEEL SACRED.

At some point I threw in the towel and decided to just drive the car wherever those darn carjackers wanted to go without complaint. Part of my reasoning for choosing a theme like sacred was that I knew it was going to be a year of transition and I wanted to be fully present for these moments. What I didn't fully realize was that it might not look like I expected. If I am honest with myself, being called in different directions than I expected caused tension and made me feel like a failure. When I recognized that certain expectations weren't being met, I finally gave in and I let life unfold naturally. Then things began to shift.

As I reflected on my year in this new light, what I saw was suddenly very sacred. Instead of seeing all of the goals that weren't accomplished or didn't happen the way I hoped, I began to see something else emerge. I saw myself completely immersed in this year of change. My oldest was looking at medical schools, going on a mission trip to Haiti, no longer living at home in the summer and working. My middle one finished her 10th and final season of ski racing, graduated high school, decided to defer college and pursue music across the country and moved. My youngest played volleyball, lost the constant companionship of her sisters and began her final year of middle school. My hubby and I had time together...alone.

I didn't do a lot of training. I didn't run the races I expected. I didn't accomplish all of the goals I set out for myself, but I was present for all of the big moments and you know what? It turns out my year was pretty sacred afterall.

HEADPHONES ANYONE?

"Be thankful for all the rude, obnoxious, and difficult people you meet in life. They serve as important reminders of how NOT to be."

—Anonymous

During certain seasons of my life I have traveled quite a bit. One of the things I like most is meeting people, and travel can facilitate a friendship like nothing else. However, occasionally, you should just wear your headphones.

In order to save time, sanity, and my own dignity I will condense my two-and-a-half-hour flight into a few highlights. Upon boarding the very small, bordering on claustrophobic, plane to Chicago, a man—whom I will call Mr. D—informed me that his seat was beside mine. Within minutes he inquired about my marital status and exactly how long I had been married. He was aghast at how anyone could possibly be married for 23 years as he could not comprehend being with one person that long. He then offered that while he was currently married and had two children, ages 2 and 4, he would be divorcing his wife when his children turned 18. He also informed me that he didn't like to wear his wedding ring as it was uncomfortable. As an added bonus he let me know that women don't care if he is married or not as marriage is apparently not a deterrent to "hooking up." As you can see, Mr. D was a real charmer. While I was appalled by pretty much everything that came out of Mr. D's mouth, I was already imagining telling this story to my family so I forged ahead.

Mr. D was also very informative about male behavior. He took it upon himself to educate me about "husbands who travel for business." He wanted me to know that all men who travel cheat on their wives. When I disagreed, he said, "So, you are telling me that you believe your husband has never cheated on you?"

I looked at him and said, "Look at me. I am the best thing that ever happened to my husband. He would be a fool to cheat on me and no, I don't believe for a second that he has ever strayed."

Mr. D smiled, but had apparently run out of educational tips on my marriage as he moved on to other topics like the ages of my daughters.

Later, Mr. D told me he would like to stay in Chicago for the night and pretend he wasn't a husband and father. Something tells me he won't have to pretend for very long.

As I disembarked from my little plane trip from hell I did not look over to tell Mr. D how much I enjoyed talking to him. I felt pretty sure he knew the answer. I was wrong. Mr. D chased me down in the airport to tell me how much he loved conversing with me during the flight and that he hoped I had fun at the funeral.

Oh, Mr. D you really are a charmer.

Note to Mrs. D: You might want to put a leash on that stray dog of yours and while you are at it you might think about an electric collar for when he misbehaves!

LOWI
&G

THE HUSBAND

*"A wedding anniversary is the celebration of
love, trust, partnership, tolerance, and tenacity.
The order varies for any given year."*

—Paul Sweeney

I am not exactly sure when it happened, but my husband has decided that he has done enough. When I say he has done enough, I mean he wrongly assumes that after 21 years he has met his quota for compliments, anniversary gifts, Valentine flowers, and birthday gifts.

I noticed something was amiss at Christmas. He called me one afternoon to ask when I would be home because he wanted me to go see some pottery with him.

What? Who has abducted my husband and replaced him with Clinton Kelly? Pottery?

I arrived home and sure enough, he whisked me into town to see some fabulous pottery that he thought would be a great addition to our mountain home. I agreed. We picked some out and he began talking about a spreadsheet and time-frame. What?

My husband had returned, and the conversation went something like this:

Husband: "So, I was thinking I could buy you a couple of pieces for Christmas, and there is a lot here, so it's going to take awhile to collect."

Me: "Yes, it's a little pricey, and there is a lot here."

Husband: "Well, I looked into the person who makes it and she isn't going to retire anytime soon, so I have time."

Translation for those of you having difficulty following along: I have every gift-giving holiday mapped out—on a spreadsheet—for the next five years. I don't have to give it any thought whatsoever! Isn't it great?

Hmmm. Yes? I do like the pottery and it's not like I really need anything. It's just nice to know that your husband is thinking about you. It's a great idea. We picked out a few pieces and voilá they were under the tree Christmas morning.

Let's fast-forward one week to our anniversary. Right now, you are thinking you know where this is going, right? Nope!

Nothing. That's right folks, not even a card. What? Where is the pottery? Where is the love? I don't want to translate incorrectly here, so let me just give you a direct quote from my lovely husband of 21 years:

Husband: "Well, last year was a big year. It was 20 years and we went to a hotel and stuff and I did buy you a bracelet. Oh and I just bought you pottery for Christmas."

Me: "We did have a beautiful 20-year celebration, last year. So you really didn't get me a card?"

There was some stuttering, but ultimately there was no card or pottery. Really, it's OK, I didn't need or want anything. It's just nice knowing your husband of 21 years thought of you long enough to NOT purchase a card.

Now, don't get me wrong. It's not about the gifts. It's about what has happened in the last year. Is there an unwritten guy code that says,

"Hey bro, if you make it to 20 years, you are golden. No need to go to too much trouble anymore, she isn't leaving you, you got this!"

WHISPER WORTHY

"If you cannot get rid of the family skeleton,
you may as well make it dance."

—George Bernard Shaw

Every family has its quirks, eccentricities, and down-right bat shit craziness. Ours is no different except that, possibly, we're gifted. We have our lingo, our unspoken rules and some topics have been unequivocally deemed: whisper-worthy.

Whisper-what?

Whisper-worthy, you read that right.

In our family there are certain topics, situations, people or illnesses that fall into this category. They are so taboo, unfortunate or offensive that they need not be spoken at an audible level for fear that random stray dogs might hear.

There really aren't parameters on what is whisper-worthy per sé. It's just that one or more family members needs to whisper about this topic in conversation and word, or whisper, spreads pretty quickly.

An example of the randomness of said worthiness is when I adopted a vegan diet a few years ago. I was often asked if I was still eating "vegetables" (with a disapproving hush). Ironic as my grandparents lived on a farm and grew masses of vegetable gardens over the years. I hope you're laughing 'cause it's funny.

As you can imagine, if vegetables in your diet are being whispered about, the really serious things in life totally get the near-silent treatment. In fact, those things we may not speak of at all; at least not directly. Those are the topics that we talk around and pretend nobody knows about, but we're all talking about in code.

We are a real covert bunch, especially since none of us apparently can really keep a secret. And then there are the "why-are-we-whispering-about-this" topics, like when "weather" is coming. We might have to whisper about that.

Sometimes, I wonder, do other families whisper about the unmentionables? Or is this like the wiggy-tail holders (what others call ponytail holders)? Or the barking at the cold? Or the not eating raw cookie dough? You know, something only our brand of crazy does!

As I said, we're gifted.

UNLOAD YOUR BAGGAGE

"Letting go isn't about having the courage to release the past; it's about having wisdom to embrace the present."

—Steve Maraboli

like to think that as I age I will gain some wisdom or at the very least I will make new mistakes instead of the same ones over and over. Some people just run around in the world operating as proverbial sage to all the other, by comparison, idiots.

I will fully admit and attest to the role of idiot in this scenario.

As the Dalai Lama says, when you are speaking you are talking about what you already know. When you are listening there is the chance to learn something new...

One of my personal gurus right now is a 75-year-old art curator who is more fabulous than you can properly conjure. In fact, in a word she is more: more fun, more knowledgeable, more entertaining, more alive, more aware than maybe anyone I've ever met.

She's living an examined life. She knows what she's doing, where she's been, and she's not only made peace with it, she's found meaning. And she shares it freely.

She must have sensed some of my trepidation about a new project because she offered up this at her front door:

Stand in the present without your past, without your baggage.

Who could you be?

What could you do?

Without hesitation I said, "Anything! I'd be free."

Mind blown.

Sails filled.

Unburdened.

I thought I was speechless after that, but fear not... I called Lowi. She was being the dutiful exerciser so I left her a voicemail with this luminous guidance.

I share so you, too, can have that moment of spontaneous knowing. Yours will be different than mine, and that's the way it should be.

Go ahead, stand up. You need to stand up for this.

Feel your feet on the Earth.

Ask yourself, "Who could I be? What could I do?"

There. Marching orders have arrived.

Go on, get to it.

PART 4

KICKING AND SCREAMING TOWARDS GRATITUDE

"Gratitude unlocks the fullness of life. It turns what we have into enough, and more. It turns denial into acceptance, chaos to order, confusion to clarity. It can turn a meal into a feast, a house into a home, a stranger into a friend."

—Melody Beattie

CHRISTMAS CAKES

"Practicing gratitude through the chaos of life helps us to seek the sunshine even when the clouds threaten to overtake it all."

—Lowi & G

A friend once asked me where I thought the root of our gratitude stemmed from. I am not sure I had ever really thought about it in quite that way. I usually thought about gratitude in terms of finding true joy and happiness. G and I grew up in church so, of course, being thankful for the gifts and blessings we received was ingrained in our DNA, but it was also more than that. You know that game you played when you were young where you say the first word that pops into your mind when someone says another word? Well, it went something like this:

Gratitude = Christmas Cakes.

This was something that I hadn't thought about in more than 20 years, but the thought quickly blanketed me with the sweetest memory.

Our mom owned a bakery and for as long as I can remember she would make about a million cakes, give or take a few, and we would deliver them on Christmas Eve to EVERYONE. Why? Well, because she wanted to do something special for people and this was her gift, but also because she wanted to show each and every one one of them how much they were appreciated. Now, she could have had one of us girls just run up, ring the bell, give wishes for a Merry Christmas, and move on to the next house, but she didn't. She made all three of us girls go with her to each house and all of us would deliver the cake and visit with each person or family.

Lest you think we were some kind of angels, we whined about it the entire time we were loading the van with cakes! When you are a pre-teen the last thing you want to do on Christmas Eve is visit with a bunch of people and make small talk. All we really wanted to do was get to our grandparents' house for the main event with our cousins.

I must have been about 11 or 12 years old when I began to understand the real importance of this ritual. There was an elderly woman from our church who we would visit periodically. On this particular Christmas Eve she was so happy to see us. During the visit she pointed to a mirror and said, "Do you see the finger-prints on that mirror? Those are from the last time you visited. Everyday I look at that mirror and it makes me think of all of you."

She had intentionally not cleaned that mirror since our last visit. In that moment I understood that this ritual had nothing to do with cakes and everything to do with gratitude.

And so a seed was planted to be tended to another day.

HAPPINESS JARS

*"While we are focusing on fear, worry or
hate, it is not possible for us to be experiencing
happiness, enthusiasm or love."*

—Bo Bennett

One year in early January, I read a post on Facebook from author Elizabeth Gilbert about happiness jars. All these awesome, creative folks were sending her photos of their happiness jars—containers that were beautified in ways you can't imagine. The idea was to fill the jar over the next 365 days with all the moments that were memorable, happy, and as I started referring to it: jar-worthy.

Then on New Year's Eve you crack open the jar and read through all the happy entries you've entrusted to the jar over the year. I, for one, am of the persuasion that when the end of a year rolls around I am so over it that I long for a shiny new year. I start to think about the year we are ending as last year's sweater that I have spilled umpteen different things on and it's now stained. It also smells and, frankly, you don't want to be seen with it.

But the happiness jar really changed all that. After I rolled through all those pieces of paper, ticket stubs, post-it notes and written-on napkins that had been hanging out in the jar, I was able to relive all that happened in those 365 days. Sure each year has its fair share of heartbreak, sorrow and disappointment. But consistently on December 31st I find myself sitting with all of these memories committed to paper that reminded me the year was also filled with love, giggles, accomplishment, and true joy.

So, I write it down or I'll forget. I write it down, and I savor it!

These are just two of the reasons that happiness jars are vital if you want to grow gratitude and you are not by nature a warm fuzzy. You might be, like me, more of a who-the-hell-has-been-drinking-from-my-once-full-glass type of person.

At least that's why I do it. I am not someone who innately counts blessings. I am thankful, but I also need a good, sturdy nudge on occasion. I am a sarcastic soul and that sharp wit, sadly, requires a lens more focused on what's wrong, what's weird, not what's amazing. I am more of a bracer, a wait for the other shoe girl. I like to be prepared. So this whole embrace-the-world, swing-the-door-to-your-heart-wide-open way of living is a conscious effort for me.

I do warm up—don't get me wrong—and once I do, and you've learned the secret handshake, the password, AND you have the decoder ring, I am pretty much an open book. But if I want to keep you at arm's length, we won't even pinky swear. Ever!

While that might be marked on my DNA some-where, I strongly believe we can change. We can hone other skills. We can be different if we want.

And I want... I want to be someone who, without thought, hugs someone that I don't know upon meet-ing them because it feels like good heart sense. I want to end the day regaling my cats (yes, I talk to them) about all the good stuff that happened and not all that was more like cleaning their litter boxes.

I want happy and grateful, to be my default position instead of sassy, salty—and OK I will say it—sarcastic. And the happiness jar helps me to do that. Not every second, not even every day, but more. More is good. More is better in this circumstance. Some weeks I do well. Other times I drift. But I keep coming back.

My hope is I not only add the items that I have ren-dered jar-worthy, but also adding the "every day" items as well. The truth of it all is that every day has happiness. Even in the face of sadness there are small mo-ments that touch us with hope and glimmer of the joy that's to return. As Ali Edwards shares on her website and work on "Week in the Life," the moments you miss when your life changes are the everyday rituals or peo-ple you've grown to expect.

A few years ago, I wouldn't have written down how it touches my heart when my cat, Parsley, presses her nose to mine and purrs. It reminds me that while we may have given her a home, she's really been the one to give us the gift.

I want the jar to be a living testament to all the greatness in my life.

In my constant effort to be better, live better, expe-rience better, I sometimes take for granted that there is a lot of greatness that's already arrived safely into my life and heart.

LIVING ZEN IN REAL LIFE

*"By letting it go it all gets done. The world is
won by those who let it go. But when you try and
try. The world is beyond the winning."*

—Lao Tzu

As a mom, life can get a little chaotic. In my attempts to go with the flow and embrace life where it is I am always looking for new ways to breathe more deeply and be grateful.

Once upon a time I took a meditation class. It was supposed to help me stay focused and keep some perspective when the trivial threatened to bombard my senses. It worked...for the 12 weeks I was actually taking the class. That's how self-improvement works with me. I have these great ideas and I get super motivated and then life slowly takes over. I am one of those people who needs a one-to-one life motivator every second of the day.

This is where G usually steps in to try to save me from myself...I mean, help me. She thought it would be a great idea for us to try a Kriya Meditation. For this particular meditation, you practice for 40 days in a row for nine minutes per day. The trick is the position. You have one arm pointed up and outward while the other arm is behind you pointed downward while seated in the lotus position. Sounds easy enough, but holding your arms in that position for nine minutes proved more difficult than I imagined. The other thing that proved difficult was the company that decided to join me for these meditation sessions. My three daughters decided that they, too, would like to meditate with me in a group setting. So, the first night we sat in a circle, assumed the position and proceeded to meditate... for about three seconds. That's when the laughter and jokes began.

The conversation went something like this among my daughters:

Are we getting zen?

Is this a zen circle?

Let's call it a znircle!

Why are we pointing to the stars?

This looks like some kind of crazy worship circle.

Are we calling E.T. home?

Are we waiting for the mother ship to come?

Are you sure we aren't signaling for the aliens to come and take us home?

How long has it been?

My arms are tired.

Wait, what's my back arm supposed to be doing?

Has it been nine minutes yet?

The second night, the dog decided to get in on the action and more laughter ensued.

While we all ended up in a pile on the floor laughing, it wasn't exactly how I imagined my new meditation practice.

Something similar happened when I tried to broach the subject of making happiness jars. My sassy, snarky family felt like they had some better ideas about savoring gratitude. Introducing the idea of keeping little jars of happy was more complicated than I anticipated:

Me: "Hey guys, I know you will probably think this is another pie in the sky idea, but I think it's really important to keep gratitude a priority in our lives."

Husband: *Trying not to laugh, but all out laughing...*

Girls: *Rolling their eyes simultaneously like synchronized swimmers!*

Me: (Ignoring all of their negativity.) "Seriously, I think we should all have a happiness jar this year. It's very simple. We just have to write down on a piece of paper when something special, joyful or happy occurs, along with the date and put it in the jar."

Husband & Girls: *Laughing...*

Me: "I'm serious, it's not that difficult and then on New Year's Eve we can look through the jars and think about all of the happy moments we had."

Husband: "I think I need a jar about something a little less than joy, laughing more... Maybe something along the lines of a 'Least Negative Jar.'"

Girls: *Still laughing and encouraging the antics of their father.*

Me: "OK, fine. I am making myself a 'Happiness Jar' and I am making you a, 'Least Negative Thing That Happened to Me Today Jar.'"

Middle Daughter: "Can we have a money jar for every time someone is negative? And then the least negative person gets to collect the money at the end of the week... you know they say the middle child is always the most positive so maybe we can just call it my allowance."

Husband & Girls: *Rolling onto the floor laughing...*

Me: *Laughing because I know really, really deep down they love the idea.*

So, how did it end? I made my oldest daughter a "Happiness Jar" for her to take to back to college. She thanked me and sent me a photo.

And?

I made a "Family Happiness Jar" and a "Least Negative Thing that Happened to Me Jar." Regardless of what we call it, it's all about gratitude.

These are the real moments of zen, people. I have to take it where I can get it! I am not sure I will ever attain the peace, fresh start, focus or moment of zen that I crave, but the znircle was fun and we all have a jar!

JINGLE JANGLE

"Let your practice be a celebration of life."

—Seido Lee deBarros

A few years ago, Lowi was doing a presentation on Gratitude. She asked me if I would participate in an exercise of starting the day with 10 bracelets on my left wrist and as the day went on every time I acted in gratitude and kindness I could move one to the right wrist. When I did the opposite I had to move it back. It was like walking around with your own personal gratitude abacus calculating your grace, your missteps, and your colossal failures.

I made an entrance everywhere I went with these cheap bracelets banging against one another. As a personal trainer and yoga teacher, jewelry is not a big part of my life so it got attention as you can imagine.

I had the punishment, I mean opportunity, each day to answer the question as to what I was doing with ALL of these bracelets. Soon I not only was walking around with my thankfulness abacus, but the world got to see how "grateful" I was or wasn't. Yep, it was special.

In fact, one night during a yoga class they were a bit disruptive so I took them off and set the respective right and left wrist piles at the front of my mat. As I took them off I made a disparaging comment about them and my class quickly admonished me and requested I move a bracelet back to the left wrist pile.

Nothing like instant karma in your yoga class, right?

All week long these little sparkling delights beckoned me to be kind, to be grateful, to be the person I say I want to be. There was lots of mental complaining and kvetching that went on, but after a few days it started to grow on me. At first, I felt like I might be losing my sarcastic edge and that made me a little panicky because really who am I without a quick, well-placed retort and a sideways glance and crooked grin? Could I find out?

Maybe with my eyes squinted looking through my fingers I could... sorta... maybe, but since I promised Lowi I couldn't just drop this "gratitude thing" as I wanted to. I had to follow through. She is my big sister so really when you're not the big sister that's reason enough... even if you are an adult.

I persevered and I didn't die. Not even close. Was I an instantly gracious and more kind person? No. Was I still a smart ass? You better believe it.

But I was thinking about gratitude. I was letting the idea bang around in my head like those bracelets banged around on my arms for seven days. And like most things, if you beat against the resistance long enough, you get in. OK sometimes you get a headache, but then you get in.

That's the first time I considered gratitude as a practice. And less like something that just runs into you sideways when good stuff happens.

Since that experiment, I have on some years busted out the bracelets the seven days leading up to Thanksgiving as a booster shot. Those who I have known for a long time recognize them, and I think they find the returning ritual enjoyable too. They start thinking about their gratitude or at least they are thinking how grateful they'll be when I stop wearing those clanging, loud bracelets. But gratitude all the same. A win's a win.

GIVE LOVE, GET LOVE

"The love we give away is the only love we keep."

—Elbert Hubbard

It's the little things that really can make a day. It's for the little things that we are grateful. The little things really are the big things.

One day, I received a little email with a big message and a subject line that said: This Made Me Think of You.

Inside was this quote:

> *When you find people who not only tolerate your quirks, but celebrate them with glad cries of 'Me, too!' be sure to cherish them. Because those weirdos are your tribe."*
>
> —Anonymous

It only took about 30 words and I felt thankful, grateful, appreciated, and understood. All that received in a short amount of time and word exchange. It wasn't even really a word exchange, but an energy exchange.

GOOD ENERGY = GOOD ENERGY. BAD ENERGY = SOMETHING ELSE.

Give love, get love.

COMPASSION RECEIVED

"Love and compassion are necessities, not luxuries.
Without them, humanity cannot survive."

—Dalai Lama

I had the opportunity, thanks to the kindness and understanding of another, to be in a place of gratitude that could have so easily been a place of anger and frustration.

I was leaving the parking lot of my local grocery store and I almost ran right into another car as I pulled out of my parking space. Honestly, I am not sure how it happened. I wasn't distracted, on the phone, or doing anything but "driving while human."

The other driver was quite upset although by hitting the brakes quickly we did avoid a near fender-bender. However, when we made eye contact I said, "I am sorry, my fault." She clearly understood my apology and replied with, "It's OK."

BOOM I got compassion!

She let me off the hook for being human and that we all make mistakes. I waived back and said, "thank you."

There, as simple as that, we both had the opportunity to extend compassion, receive compassion, and I am certainly grateful. It was a small exchange and yet it could've easily ended in angry gestures, cars speeding off, and negative emotions. But instead, other than feeling a bit like an idiot for my poor driving in that moment, I drove away feeling hopeful.

SCARCITY, JOY, AND ROLLER COASTERS

"We can spend our entire lives in scarcity . . . just waiting for for the other shoe to drop and wondering when it will all fall apart. Or, we can lean into the uncertainty and be thankful for what we have in that precious moment. When I'm standing at the crossroads of fear and gratitude, I've learned that I must choose vulnerability and practice gratitude if I want to know joy. I'm not sure that it will ever be easy for me, but I have learned to trust this practice. For that, I give thanks!"

—Brené Brown

A t certain points in my life I have found myself worrying about things over which I have no control. I would wake up in a mindset of scarcity and wondering when it was all going to fall apart. I was always waiting for the other shoe to drop. I found that these feelings intensified as my kids were getting older and moving away. During a particularly difficult transition, one of my daughters had a lot going on in her life. It was exciting, new, and scary at times. In fact, this transition was so big, so new, so exciting, that I found myself questioning the outcome and the uncertainty of her path.

In the simplest terms it became a question of embracing scarcity or joy.

When I shared these feelings with her, she said, "I am taking each day as it comes with all of its opportunities and excitement. I am not worrying about tomorrow and what may or may not come. I am just loving everything about today!"

That is what choosing joy over scarcity looks like.

Then sometimes joy and scarcity arrive together.

Right after we had this discussion two young ski racers, ages 19 and 20, lost their lives to an avalanche while free skiing in Austria. I didn't know these young men although it's possible that we have been on the same mountain at the same time, as my aforementioned daughter was a competitive ski racer for years.

We have lived in that world and know a lot of young people the same ages as these two young men. The youngest man had just been asked to go on this trip to Austria and ski with the U.S. Development Ski Team.

I have been thinking about the joy and excitement of his family and friends because we know so many who have the same aspirations. Being on the U.S. Ski Team is what all of these young skiers are working toward. One week they were celebrating his accomplishments and the next week mourning his loss.

As a parent or family member, how do you reconcile so much joy with this incredible sorrow?

I think Dr. Jim Taylor said it best in his article about this ski racing tragedy, *"For all of us, there is the awareness that life can be so fragile sometimes. Yet to live life safely, or expect our children to, is to live half a life that lacks meaning, fulfillment, and joy. Only by living on the edge where, sadly, there are risks, can life be fully embraced and enjoyed."*

So, I am choosing to live authentically, practice gratitude, and live in the moment. I am not going to stand on the outside watching. I am going to get in line, ride the roller coaster, and hang on for the ride. I'm ready to take it ALL in.

THANKS FOR THE SOLE

"I don't run because I love the feeling of running. I run because it makes me love the feeling of living."

—Bonnie Pfiester

I had to say goodbye. I have a hard time with farewells, but especially when I'm parting ways with ones who've:

Supported me.

Carried me.

Cushioned my hard steps along the way.

Protected me through my stumbles and propelled me to my greatest personal goals.

We spent countless, untold hours together without a single complaint or falter. I said goodbye to my running shoes.

My two pairs of sole friends did their job, and leaving them behind is a mix of emotions.

I am always excited to buy new shoes. What girl isn't? But I also feel kinda sad when that time rolls around. These shoes, in particular, have been with me through my hardest, most challenging and telling moments. They were with me every step, literally, through nearly 200 race miles.

But they were with me during the less exciting parts too: the training. They got me through the all-day slugfests out in the snow; endless ice-filled days that lead me to the treadmill; the days where I didn't want to run, but I didn't want to quit either.

There aren't many people or things you can be sure will stay with you throughout but the shoes did.

After so many miles, around 800, you know how the shoe feels, supports you, and how it likes to commune with the ground. That matters when you're a runner. But like many relationships, they have a beginning and an end. When they've completed their job and taught you what you needed to learn, it's OK to let go. It's OK to move toward the next lesson.

It's time for new shoes to carry me.

So thanks to my sole sisters, who I am retiring, and welcome to those I haven't yet met. I am sure we'll be SFF before we know it. (That's Sole Friends Forever, if you don't speak my language.)

FLAWED OR FABULOUS

"There is nothing more rare, nor more beautiful,
than a woman being unapologetically herself;
comfortable in her perfect imperfection. To me,
that is the true essence of beauty."

—Steve Maraboli

I found myself staring at my gratitude journal and feeling blank. I was running the list of things for which I was ungrateful. (I will shield you from the list.) Hmmmm, not the best start to a day, right?

It felt like the list of things that were "broken" had gotten rather lengthy. I was questioning if it's realistic to even think that this list will ever be fully checked off. Let's be honest, the list of broken stuff will always be around and it all probably won't ever get fixed.

And in a lot of cases the F in our Flaw List is really what makes us fabulous!

Being flawed is fabulous? Well, yes and no.

I have been known to get myself in a wee bit of trouble because I have a bit of a sassy mouth. Most of the time I don't consider that to be a very delightful feature. However, if I were to ask my husband or a few of my close friends it's likely to be one of the first things they'd say they embrace about me. It's not that they don't see how opening my mouth to make room for my foot isn't at times, well um, uncomfortable. Instead, it's that they like me or love me for it, or in spite of it. Who knows?

My perceived flaw is part of why they like me. Does that mean I should say any old thing that comes to mind? In case you aren't sure let me give you a definitive no!

But, we can take a lighter look at some of our quirks and instead find ways to be thankful for them while doing our best to keep the crazier parts in check when necessary.

Who knows what you'll find or what will make you laugh?

MY PERSON

"She's my person. If I murdered someone, she's the
person I'd call to help me drag the corpse across
the living room floor. She's my person."

—Grey's Anatomy

Do you ever feel like you are just walking around trying to sort out the crazy that is running through
your head? This happened to me recently (OK, it happens a lot) and I knew I needed my person, but she was
busy so I continued to try to crawl out of the rabbit
hole I had fallen into. While I wasn't entirely successful, I was functioning at a level that would not make
anyone take a second glance. Then she texted me. She
has that sixth sense. She called me and we shared what
was going on in both of our lives.

Don't get me wrong I share with a lot of people, but
this woman, she can take anything I dish out and there

will be no judgment. It's what I imagine confession would be like if I were Catholic without any Hail Marys. It soothes my soul and I feel free from the burdens that were weighing me down prior to our talk. I literally can say anything without a filter. I never have to look through the lens first and say to myself, "Eh, that might be a little too much information to share with another human being." Nope, she will laugh with me or cry with me because she knows exactly what I am feeling.

We met when our oldest children were beginning fourth grade, and we have now been friends for 12 years. From our first conversation we have been in total sync. She was the first person my oldest spent the night with that I didn't really know. It started as a simple after-school play date and turned into a reluctant sleepover. I remember my husband saying, "It will be fine. They sounded nice on the phone and they are at their grandparents having dinner. How horrible can they be?" Well, in my mind they could have been really horrible. All I could think about all night was that they had just moved here from Texas and they probably were carrying concealed weapons and had an arsenal under their bed!

The next morning as early as I saw fit I called the mom to make sure my child was, in fact, still alive. Immediately, I told her I had never let my child stay anywhere that a full background check had not been performed and that while I was remiss this time I hoped she didn't hold it against me...if, in fact, my child was still alive. OK, maybe I didn't say all of that, but it was implied and she got the message.

After our hellos she put me at ease by saying, "Hey, I know we haven't actually met but don't worry, we don't have any guns in the house and there are no older brothers." This was the beginning of a beautiful relationship as we instinctively knew what the other needed to hear. This back and forth has continued through the years and very quickly we realized this was not by chance. It was, as she likes to call it, "divine intervention" that brought us together. We have lived very parallel lives over these last 12 years and I could never have survived without her support, her laugh, and her genuine, loving spirit. Oh, and the little bottles of tequila she leaves on my front porch occasionally.

Reach out and nurture those friendships. You never know when you might need them to help you move a corpse across the living room floor.

LOWI
&G

EYE-ROLLING

"Joy is the simplest form of gratitude."

—Karl Barth

During one of our family vacations, I embarked on yet another gratitude experiment with the family. The plan was to have everyone state one thing that made them happy that day, three things they were grateful for, and to initiate a random act of kindness. Well, we weren't successful in sticking to the plan every single night for the two weeks, but there still were some revelations.

As always there was eye-rolling and laughter at the thought of doing any coordinated activity that did not necessarily involve the sun and the beach. I also had the whining about not wanting to do it and, of course, the gratitude for "being alive, breathing, and I can't think of anything else" answers. However, most of the time when I reminded them that we were, in fact, going to do it they followed along. As the vacation entered its second week, the gratitude and happy moments were much easier to come by as we settled into actually all being in one space. There was far less eye-rolling, more patience amongst one another, and dare I say they were enjoying being together.

I began to notice the sweet thank yous, greetings, door-holding, and smiles they freely gave to strangers on the street. The biggest revelation though came on the nights we discussed our moments of happiness and gratitude. These were the nights that laughter filled the house as we went to bed. The next morning also revealed smiling faces ready for another day in paradise.

A year later, I asked my oldest to recall this experience. I was curious and hopeful that the experiment had somehow made an impression on her. She immediately responded, "Oh yeah, I remember that. I know at the time we laughed a lot, but I think it brought us closer together. We were bonding over our common gratitude. We would literally lay in bed laughing and thinking about what we were grateful for each day. Also, for me, it has made me think about not only the things that I am grateful for, but the people in my life. I make a point to tell my friends that I am grateful for their friendship."

You might be wondering about what the other two had to say about this experience. Well, let's just say I was so happy about this response that I didn't want to press my luck.

LIFE CYCLES

*"There are far better things ahead
than those we leave behind."*

—C.S. Lewis

You hear devastating news and everything in your body, your mind, everything says no. It's not always direct. It's not always obvious. But if you look closely, if you're paying attention—you see it.

The resistance, denial, pushing away, pulling away, running away.

It might just be our attention or body language. It may feel like our cells are trying to run from the knowledge. But like water on pavement, it eventually finds every crack, every crevice, and it does what it does—sinks in.

I wouldn't call it acceptance at first. It's acknowledgement.

I see you over there.
That new wrinkle in life.
That new obstacle.
That newly realized fear.
And I want you to know, we're not friends.
We won't ever be.
It's not personal, it just is.

That's how it goes with news you don't want. And it comes all the time. And it's never a good time. It's important to remember that many people are struggling—especially during times when it seems we should be celebrating—like during the holidays. Just because the calendar says it's time to celebrate and be grateful doesn't mean that our heart suddenly feels it. There likely isn't a family out there who hasn't been affected by some kind of illness, discomfort or tragedy.

Why? Because life cycles, it moves. It's a living entity, and it's always changing.

And we can hardly bear it.

It's not easy, but focusing your attention on the positive really does make a difference over time. If we are honest, wouldn't we rather be living in a place of gratefulness than bitterness?

The next time you are up pacing at night because you are worried and can't sleep, notice the light of the moon, the snow, the wind, the quiet peacefulness.

When your pain and stress subside for an hour, notice and acknowledge the ease in which you rest during this time.

There is a place for sadness, grief and anger. And it will find you. It darkens all our doors during the seasons of life. It's just not where we want to focus our time and energy. We need to acknowledge that we are hurting and let our emotions out. It's good for the soul. So hug your family and friends and have a good cry, but then take a deep breath, release the negative, and see the positive that is before you.

Gratitude can be a perspective-changer if you choose to put it into practice. When you focus on what you have versus what's lacking you suddenly realize you have abundance. In the darkness we find something to move toward, we can say yes. It cycles on.

CONFLICTING EMOTIONS

"To be human and to be adult means constantly to be in the grip of opposing emotions, to have daily to reconcile apparently conflicting tensions. I want this, but need that. I cherish this, but I adore its opposite too."

—Stephen Fry

"I have a lot to be thankful for." I heard this statement spoken wistfully by more than one person in a short period of time. It wasn't until I heard the second person say it more than once in a conversation that I realized I was actually hearing guilt.

The juxtaposition was uncanny and unmistakable.

Both of these women were going through their own hardships. And while I know them both to be quite grateful and appreciative, the truth of it was that life was difficult.

What they were not saying, what they were holding back was: I hate this! I don't want to be living this. I don't want to be enduring this. I want out!

And because they had gifts running alongside their challenges the honesty of how they felt sounded wrong, so guilty gratitude was their default.

Guilt-laden gratitude? I feel confident that's not what gratitude journals and practices are intending to cultivate, but I saw how they got there. We have this idea that gratitude and an "attitude" can't live in the same space. They can.

We have the word bittersweet in our vocabulary for a reason. Life isn't linear and it sure doesn't always meet at clean congruences.

Love and loss at times arrive together. Pain and relief can be constant companions. Light and dark are frequently co-pilots. So why not hell and gratitude?

A few weeks after this, I visited a colleague who had metastatic breast cancer. The disease was progressing and her treatments were palliative in nature. During my time with her and several other friends she shared her thoughts about cancer, how she doesn't like the metaphor of battling cancer or that someone is often deemed as "losing" his or her battle to cancer when they die. She was adamant that a death to cancer is not losing.

More than 10 years after her initial diagnosis she was well-versed in the subject. I am sure more so than she ever dreamed or would ever want to be.

She lamented that people don't want to hear about how hard it is to have cancer. She said they don't want to hear that you're struggling. They want you to be positive and optimistic in every moment.

I thought to myself, "Well, hell, if you can't talk about a bad day when you have cancer that's likely going to take your life, when can you?"

The more I listened to her share her experience I started to have this sinking feeling that I may have done something similar in my effort to be supportive.

When my aunt was diagnosed I was trying to be upbeat and positive, but it was dawning on me that I was instead unintentionally dismissive. I was afraid of her fear because I thought I needed to solve it. All I needed to do was hear it, acknowledge it, be with her in the fear.

But we do learn.

In the midst of these many weeks that seemed littered with diagnoses and prognoses that lurked on every corner, I started to do better. One night I looked at a struggling friend and said, "I know that you are grateful for what you have but it's OK to say this sucks! It's OK to say, I am so tired of this!" At first she looked a little shocked, and then what I saw was relief.

And after that the words she spoke relayed genuine gratitude, thankfully.

Even in what were some of my friend's final days I was still learning, she was still teaching. Everyone wants to be seen, heard and know they matter. In life and in death. Gratitude and hell can live together. It's a beautiful tragedy.

LOWI
& G

LOOKING FOR WHAT'S RIGHT

*"If you don't start appreciating what's right
in front of you, you might lose it."*

—Anonymous

O ne of the greatest parts of focusing on self-love is
the idea of surrounding yourself with love:

- People who love you.

- People you love.

- Environments which feel loving.

- Participating in activities that you love.

- Telling those important people that you love them
  and how you feel.

It's funny, in February, we are often only focused on the big pronouncements of love: boxes of chocolate, roses, nice dinners. And there isn't anything wrong with that.

But lots of loving things you hear, see, and experience aren't that obvious unless you are looking for them; open to them. It doesn't always have to be big, bold gestures. And we aren't always paying attention or looking for them. It's the difference in two basic mindsets:

Looking for what's wrong or looking for what's right.

When I spent time looking for ways to be more open to this I discovered that a lot is, well, right!

It's often in the simple, little things that the "rightness" shows itself.

- Having someone reach out an un-gloved hand in below-zero weather just so they can hold yours.

- A friend wishing you luck on an event even though she can't be there.

- Receiving a card in the mail from someone you see all the time. She took the extra step to let you know she cares.

- Hearing thank you for doing a task you do every day, but your spouse or friend wanted you to know that it's noticed and appreciated.

But I easily could miss it if I wasn't paying attention. I could dismiss it if I decided it needed to be more. (And I am sure there have been many times I have overlooked it.)

It's not about making something out of nothing and pretending it's love. But think about the things that you do every day that are, on their most basic level, motivated by love.

You pack lunch for your kids or spouse (or both). Now sure you want them to eat, but when you really get down to it you spend the time because you love them.

You make sure your family has clean clothes in their closets because you love them.

You spend some time making cookies for someone for no reason... yep, you guessed it, because you love them.

If these seemingly every day things are how you express love, it's probably how those in your life send you the same message.

PART **5**

WHERE'S MY MAP?

"Not all those who wander are lost."

—J.R.R. Tolkien

NEUTRAL

"Not knowing when the dawn will come, I open every door."

—Emily Dickinson

Neutral. It's not something most of us like. Neutrality isn't as unknown as we try to pretend. It's a part of all the stages of life: childhood, tweens, teens, college, young adulthood, midlife, late life. And as much as we hate it, being in neutral has taken up more of our time than we'd like.

How many times did we wait for summer?

How long did it take for the night before the first day of school to end?

How long did it feel like it took to walk down the aisle on your wedding day?

Not as long as it took to find Mr. Right?

And the right job?

Ooh wait, you're still looking?

Yep. Neutral, it seems, is so ubiquitous we almost don't see it. It's the snake that didn't almost bite you. It's been biting you all along. You are, we are, snake-bit by neutral.

Crap.

Maybe neutral is actually suspense, we just don't know it yet. Neutral is suspense?

Not always, but what feels like stuck in neutral, revving the engine is what college looks like before your degree. It's all about contracting and expanding.

Neutral is the waiting space you need until the time is right. But at other times neutral is where you land when you don't know what else to do, or when you're too scared to do what you know needs doing, or you're so mixed up, distracted and turned inside out that holding still feels like the only choice.

I have often fallen into the latter. I've been mixed up, distracted, and turned so far inside out that I feel as if I'm right side out again. For the longest time, I was waiting for when I'd feel like a grown up in order to make big decisions. I kept thinking that confidence, knowledge, and maybe even wisdom would befall me.

It took a good long while before I realized nobody is a grown up. Nobody has any damn clue what they are doing. We're all still about 12 years old, but with a driver's license, a mortgage, and a job.

That revelation was equal parts relief and terrifying.

Relief because I wasn't behind. And terrifying because it's a part of life.

A MANDATE

"Life begins at the end of your comfort zone."

—Neale Donald Walsch

L owi and I were both on our own collective journeys to alternate locations in the United States. Both transported, in a way, to a preview of what our lives could be like in the near future.

Lowi seeing her middle daughter, Sydney, visit a college that would take her far from home. And I was attending a conference that hosted speakers who inspired and challenged me to figure out if I could be more of myself in this life.

I've often been stumbling into the idea of Living Big. I have willingly taken on challenges that pushed me out of my comfort zone. And at times, I have been unceremoniously thrust into them.

I didn't handle the pressure well all the time, but in fleeting moments of clarity, I tried to hang onto the idea that I want to Live Big and not small.

To be clear, to me living big isn't about having fame, public accolades or recognition. It's, instead, about showing up in my life for the people that matter, myself included. It's about not shying away from the things that scare the hell out of me. But, instead, doing them anyway and finding out just exactly how tough, courageous, or adaptable I can be.

It's about trying to not let any moment go un-lived if I can help it. Now, of course, I still have to go to work, do the laundry, and clean the shower and other tasks. I am not suggesting that every moment is unencumbered and fantastical. But we all know when we are honest with ourselves that there are areas in our lives where we shrink and make ourselves small so we don't have to push our boundaries or put ourselves out on a limb.

Boundaries being pushed and limb-hanging was the order of the day when I went to the Coaching in Leadership and Healthcare Conference and heard Yaël Farber speak. She is a South-African actress, director and playwright, and she is magnetic. She spoke of how her work, tackling multiple social ills through different individuals' personal struggles and horrors, is her mandate. Her mandate?

Like some folks are foodies, I am a wordie. I love words and what they can create and evoke and her use of the word "mandate" got my attention. It's a strong, powerful, unrelenting idea. And while she had much more to say that was equally thoughtful and enlightening, this idea of "what is MY mandate?" has stuck with me.

I rolled it around in my conscious mind, unconscious mind, my journal, and even in conversations with others. It's almost like this idea was haunting me, but in a positive way.

I shared this with my mom and told her how listening to Farber left me wondering about my mandate, but also making me feel like I was frittering my life away. What was I doing? How was I contributing?

My mom then tells me that she has long wanted to volunteer her time to rock babies at the local Children's Hospital. It's her way to give back for all the care her nephew—our cousin—received when he was born nearly two decades ago.

Rock babies—that's what she's called to do.

She said she would look into it the next day. But something came over me and I said, "No, let's look it up right now. We are going to go rock babies."

That got me thinking. What's my equivalent to rocking babies? Surprisingly, the answer came pretty quickly: running. It always has to do with running, right? But in this case, it isn't just running, it's my foray as a running buddy for Girls on the Run. It's a way to teach girls about self-esteem, confidence, and fun while learning to run. It was a real joy and the girls were great. It didn't take long to learn that Girls on the Run has not all that much to do with running, but instead about growing up, and figuring out who you want to be—you know all the things Lowi and I are still trying to get clear on.

Clarity can be elusive and I am still not sure exactly what my mandate is. In the meantime, I am going to be a Girl on the Run and rock babies that need to be rocked. Maybe that's enough...

TRANSFORMATION

"Without a struggle, there can be no progress."

—Frederick Douglass

Once upon a time I set out to live big and transform the life I was living. It didn't take long to figure out that transformation was going to be more difficult than I realized.

While on a two-day getaway, workshop, journey-toward-change or whatever you want to call it, I decided to buy myself something. The idea was to buy something that would be a constant reminder of the things I wanted to change.

I decided on a ring. Not just any ring. It had to be big and bold, and I knew I would know it when I saw it. Thirty minutes into my shopping (in one store), I still had not found the one. I admit, I was ready to settle when the beautiful 70-year-old with long hair and piercing blue eyes said, "Wait just a minute, I think I may have the perfect ring!" This is the moment where I know I should get out quick because it is going to be perfect and it's going to come with a price tag to match! Yes, it was beautiful and it fit perfectly. The price was a little more than I had hoped to spend on my transformation, but it was worth it because it was everything I wanted. It was big, bold, beautiful, and it spoke to me.

That was a Sunday night. A mere 48 hours into my transformation I came to realize that the ring not only spoke to me, but also to my dog. Samson had been very intrigued by my ring. He watched my hand, eyed it lovingly, and every so often lunged for it.

On the following Tuesday evening, my kitchen sink was clogged. In order to fix it, I took my rings off and set them on the counter. After fixing the sink I moved my transformation ring to the back of the counter away from the sink and did some more chores around the house.

While I was working in the kitchen, my dog jumped and put his front paws on the counter. Thinking he was after the brownies, I told him to get down and ran him out of the house. About 20 minutes later I went outside and realized Samson was chewing on something and it was clanging around in his mouth. As I approached he stood up and out dropped my RING! I was devastated. I wanted to kill the dog! At that moment, I felt anger and overwhelming sadness, but more than anything I felt how difficult change can be.

My ring spent some time at the jewelers, and I eventually began speaking to my dog again.

When I got my ring back it became the reminder that I hoped it would be and more. Sometimes, in life, just like with my ring, we have to be taken apart before we can be put back together. We will both have scars from the journey, but who said transformation was easy?

GRACE

"When you are spiritually connected, you are not looking for occasions to be offended, and you are not judging and labeling others. You are in a state of grace in which you know you are connected to God and thus free from the effects of anyone or anything external to yourself."

—Wayne Dyer

We live in a culture of instant gratification. The world is at our fingertips. At the click of a button we can have anything, learn anything, ask anything, and say anything. Sometimes it's great, but other times patience is best.

Our phones, email, text messaging, and social media sites are always blowing up and we have grown accustomed to answering. I remember when the actual phone on the wall used to ring during dinner, and we would let it ring. It wasn't a catastrophe if we didn't answer. It was more important to be present with your family. When was the last time you sat with your friends or family and were totally present?

Let me ask it another way. When was the last time you sat down with family or friends and you didn't get ahead of yourself? You know, you weren't thinking about the things you needed to do tomorrow or next week. Try it, you might find that you actually enjoy being present with the people in your life. You might even learn something.

Or how about this one? What if you wanted to say something to someone good or bad and you had to actually talk to them face to face, talk to them on the phone, maybe even send them a note in the mail? Now, I know all of these things sound ridiculous to our kids and maybe even to us, but they have value. Why? Because they take thought and patience.

It's easy to blast someone on their Facebook page or send a nasty note via text message. It's not easy to pick up the phone, hear their voice and be that nasty. It's definitely not easy to wait and see them face to face. Something happens to us. Suddenly, the other person is not just the object of our anger, but another human being who has feelings.

We see ourselves in each other.

We begin to soften, become more diplomatic and sometimes we realize we really aren't angry, we are just hurt. Let's take the time to figure out how we feel and maybe give the other person a little grace. Parents have been teaching their kids to think before they speak forever, and somewhere in the last few years we have forgotten this message.

It's time to stop and breathe. It's time to be present. It's time to give a little grace.

Be HeRe Now

RESISTANCE

"Realize deeply that the present moment is all you ever have. Make the Now the primary focus of your life."

—Eckhart Tolle

You don't have to be a Star Trek fan to have heard the saying, *"Resistance is futile."*

Stop resisting.

I had a conversation with a woman who bestows her wisdom each time we speak. We were discussing the issue of being overcommitted when she told me that the best thing to do is stop resisting. She explained that, in her opinion, the idea of resisting was wasted energy and instead we should be receiving the energy from everything we are doing; soak it all in. She believes that each commitment and encounter is an opportunity and experience that we need to take in.

I realized after this conversation that I resist a lot of things in my life. I have a tendency to worry so much about what is going to happen or what might happen that I miss out on what is currently happening. It's like when you are reading a really great book and you plow through it because you can't wait to see what happens and then you are sad when it's over. We realize when we get to the end that we might have skimmed some parts because we resisted just being where we were and enjoying the moment.

I remember being on a trip and thinking we only had three days to enjoy ourselves. I spent so much time dreading the end that I know I missed out on fully appreciating the amazingness that was happening right before me. Now, I catch myself and I stop. I take a deep breath and look around. I try to breathe in the faces, the experience, the emotion. It changes me.

Our life is not a book and we don't get to re-read, re-live or redo. Be present, consciously open yourself up, and breathe in the life and positive energy of those around you. Soak it in, experience it, and when the time comes...exhale and breathe life into the really important moments.

WIDE OPEN SPACES

"Who doesn't know what I'm talking about?
Who's never left home? Who's never struck out
to find a dream and a life of their own?"

—Wide Open Spaces, Dixie Chicks

Just as the Dixie Chicks needed "wide open spaces to find a dream and a life of their own" so do we. Or at least we thought we did when we began this journey. Now maybe we just need a bus, a very small bus with very definitive boundaries and no windows because we get distracted easily.

The problem with wide open spaces is that while you no longer feel bound by the claustrophobic confines of your life, you suddenly realize you have amnesia. You can no longer remember what or why you needed space, where it was you were trying to get to and wait... what did you do with the map?

When you set out to blaze a trail of your own you have this vision, or at least we did, of this awesome dirt trail and there would be cheerleaders from all walks of our lives cheering us on. Wrong! Choosing to run amok without a firm plan in hand is an act of defiance and people don't know what to do with it. I mean just like our mother used to say, "Nothing good can come from staying out after 11:00 p.m." Nothing good can come from deviating from the cultural norm, right?

My point is that when you decide that you need to do something different, not everyone is going to jump on your bandwagon and be happy about it. Your life choices have ripple effects and not everyone is prepared to deal with those changes.

This became abundantly clear as we maneuvered through the minefield of judgment when our middle daughter decided to load the U-Haul and move a thousand miles away after graduation.

She was relocating to pursue music in Nashville. It was a gut-wrenchingly tough decision and we took a big leap of faith by helping her make this move. She has always done things a little differently, but this was definitely not what we had expected. In our part of town you take the high school, then college, get a degree, get a job path. Graduation parties were a little tough this time around.

Friends: "Where is she going to college?"

Me: "She has decided not to go right now. She is actually moving to Nashville to pursue music."

Friends: "Oh! I'm sorry. Well.. I am sure she will go as soon as she gets this out of her system."

Me: "Maybe. I am not sure what it will look like. Maybe she will be ready to come home in three months. Maybe she will decide she wants to go to school next year. I don't know. All I know for sure is that she doesn't want to go to school right now, she wants to pursue her music and she has been blessed with a lot of amazing opportunities. God has put a lot of incredible people in her life and He has continued to open doors that we did not even see. It's a leap of faith."

A lot of people look at us like we are crazy. Some people tell us that she should go for it; no regrets. One person even said, "You're right, maybe she will be back home, but maybe she will be selling out stadiums. You never know."

So, here we are running through the tumbleweeds and wildflowers of these wide open spaces and I wonder if we have made the right choice. And then it hits me. The questioning, crossing county lines and state lines, the act of choosing to do life differently...we've already succeeded. We will always be evolving and looking for new ways and we will always be looking for wide open spaces.

Thank you to those that have stepped off the beaten path to stand with us no matter what happens.

NO MOJO

*"Corpse pose restores life. Dead parts of your
being fall away, the ghosts are released."*

—Terri Guillemets

The week after a race I tend to really lack mojo—my
magic, my spark seems to have faded to a point
where I just can't see it anymore. I don't have any real
drive to get things done or make things happen. It is
normally something that bothers me because for the
most part I am a doer. I like to get things done, cross
them off my list and feel a sense of accomplishment at
the end of the day.

As a rule, I like my days to be full; not crazy busy, but
full of good people, mostly fun work, and in general,
feeling useful.

It just so happened that after one of my races, I
found myself with a week that was less than full. I had

some clients on spring break so that opened up my schedule a bit. I opted out of all things that were optional. Let's face it—I was tired; mentally, emotionally, and physically. The kind of tired that comes from pushing yourself hard. The kind of tired that comes from digging deep. For me that's usually after an ultra run.

As always, I learned a lot, stumbled my fair share, and made it through to the other side.

But I felt called to rest, not push so hard, and possibly let it all sink in. So I went with it, not so much because I wanted to, but I really didn't have the desire to fight it. Taking it easier felt good, and it actually felt right even if my mind was a little agitated by the process.

As always happens after a few days, I woke up feeling refreshed and renewed. I worry that my motivation will never come back, but then when I'm not looking it returns.

I am all for productive, but the unproductive hours as I like to call them are equally important. So much so that I probably shouldn't call them unproductive. They're like Savasana in yoga. For those of you unfamiliar, it is the final resting pose in a yoga practice and an opportunity to rest, absorb the practice, and enjoy a few moments of stillness. These are the moments where serenity finds us, relaxation arrives, and often our best ideas descend.

The final moments of yoga are the hardest for many. The stillness appears like wasted time, silliness. But I am learning, just like in yoga, if we can embrace both our quiet, easier moments and our cacophonous, intense experiences we will receive exactly what we need.

my Best asana is savasana

GET ON THE BUS

"You can avoid most of the sorrows of life, the only requirement being that you avoid all the happiness."

—Robert Brault

Life is all about risk. When we step on the bus the first day of school, away from our mother's embrace, we risk everything we have ever known for something more. Knowledge. Friends. Hope. Independence. Confidence. Opportunities. Growth. A Greater Self-Esteem. Love. Challenge. While we don't really understand that we are embarking on this journey at age 5... we are. Sometimes we get less than what our parents hoped for. We often find Enemies. Boredom. Lack of Self-Esteem. Illness. Few Opportunities. Doubt. Walls. Fear. Broken Hearts. It's these negative side effects that can stop us in our tracks. We let the fear of these things keep us at home.

When our parents put us on the bus that first morning in kindergarten they know these things. They know we will endure hardship. They know life is not always going to be easy, but they push us up those stairs anyway. Why? Because they are crazy freaks, that's why!

OK, not really. It's because life is also beautiful and fun and if we don't go out into the big, bad world how will we ever know what is outside of our four walls?

Our parents put us on that bus because they know life is about the package deal. We can't have the good without the bad. We will never appreciate our opportunities without failure, our friends without enemies, joy without pain, and love without some heartache along the way.

Nobody likes the negative side effects of life, but as we get older I think we accept that they are a necessary part of our growth.

It's tempting sometimes to stay on the safety of the sidewalk, but we were put here to brave the bus.

MAKING THE CUT

"To be yourself in a world that is constantly trying to make you something else is the greatest accomplishment."

—Ralph Waldo Emerson

The summer before my youngest began high school we embarked on a family vacation to Florida. This was a big trip—one where we would be spending lots of quality time with extended family and we were all looking forward to it. As I look back on that trip now, maybe my youngest was looking forward to it the most. She was excited to see her cousins and it was a good distraction as she would be starting high school as soon as we returned.

We did a lot of family bonding over outdoor adventures during that trip like kayaking, jet skiing and even taking a haunted tour of the town, but the one that sticks out the most is our deep sea fishing excursion.

It promised to be exciting, and while I enjoyed the ride out to the middle of the ocean with the sun on my face and the breeze in my hair, that wasn't exactly what the excursion was about. Our goal was to catch A LOT of fish for our fish fry the next evening. In fact, my mother-in-law let us know on more than one occasion how important it was to catch plenty of fish.

How hard could it be? We were on a chartered boat. The sole purpose of this boat and its crew is to take people fishing...to catch fish. They know where the fish are because they are professionals! They do this for a living, and while weather can play a large role in the number and type of fish you might catch, these charter boats boast about never coming home empty handed.

No worries, Mimi, we got this! We will bring home the fish... maybe?

Let me just tell you at the start that I didn't catch a Barracuda, a shark or, if I am being honest, a single fish worthy of taking home. Sure, I caught some fish and every single time the "captain" would look at me and say, "Not big enough, too small—pretty, but can't keep it." It didn't take long for him to stop commenting altogether. I would get a bite, reel in my catch, and he would just take the fish off my hook and throw it back... again and again.

Meanwhile, the itty bitty cousins spent 45 minutes trying to reel in a Barracuda, not once, but twice! My

father-in-law wrangled with a shark for nearly 30 minutes before the "big one got away." The other 10 family
members (remember lots of extended family on this
trip!) just kept reeling in the "right sized" fish and
throwing them in the cooler. It became comical and
then a bit depressing after awhile. I even tried fishing
with someone else's bait just in case mine was bad. I
am not even joking when I say that I didn't get a single
bite when I used the other bait.

On the way back to shore during my drug-induced
coma…I mean, while I was drifting in and out from the
effects of my motion sickness prevention medicine, I
started thinking about my fishing experience and how
much it resembled real life. How often do we feel like
we just don't make the cut? Sometimes we feel like no
matter what we do we just aren't enough. Or maybe,
like the Barracuda, we feel like we are just too much
to handle. That's certainly how I felt that day, and how
I—and pretty much every human—has felt at one time
or another—especially when embarking on something new.

Enter high school for my youngest.

Here's the thing: when my youngest started school
at the end of summer, I thought she was more than

ready. Truth be told, she had been listening to our girl power, be YOU, be confident, strong, kind, funny, giving, humble, honest talks since she was little because of her two older sisters. She had spent years watching how to navigate the teenage halls of high school angst. Theoretically, she should have been well-versed and ready to handle anything thrown her way. Theoretically.

During her first week I asked her how she was liking high school and if she had met any new friends. Her response was, "No. And just in case you are wondering, no boys like me, they don't talk to me, they don't look at me. There is obviously something wrong with me. All of my friends have boys talking to them. Also, tomorrow they are making cuts at volleyball tryouts and I am freaking out that I am not good enough to be on the team."

I was pretty sure this wasn't the time to tell her I was extremely happy and relieved that there weren't any boys talking to her let alone looking at her.

And, it made me think about that fishing trip again. I had thought as we ventured out to sea—*We got this, Mimi! We will catch a ton of fish for the fish fry!*—simply because I thought having professionals around me would make me successful in catching the fish that we needed. Had I ever done it before? No. Did I catch fish that day? Yes. I caught a lot of beautiful fish, but they just weren't what we were looking for on that day and on that particular excursion. There was nothing wrong with any of the fish I reeled in. Some of them just needed time to grow and mature. It didn't make me feel any better about not catching the "right" fish, but it was the truth and the reality is that sometimes being patient and understanding is hard. Sometimes realizing that it just isn't your time at this moment isn't what you want to hear. Sometimes it is time to just jump in and get some practice. That might yield a great catch and it might not, but at least I was in there doing what I needed to do. I was putting forth my best even amidst the struggle.

So in the end, this is what I said to my sweet girl: "Baby, you are beautiful inside and out and I am here to tell you that those boys see you. They may not be talking to you, but trust me...they see you. Just keep being you. They might be looking at you and thinking there is no way they are good enough for YOU. Just keep being you. Don't look at your friends and think they have that special something and that you need to change in any way to be like them. Just keep being you.

And while you are being you, talk to everyone, make new friends, be confident, strong, kind, giving, funny, humble, and honest. High school isn't always easy and sometimes you are going to feel like you don't make the cut. There will be times when you don't make the team or you aren't what someone is looking for, but I promise you there will come a time when you are exactly what someone is looking for. Just keep being you."

I hope she heard me somewhere deep in her soul because while this sounds good in theory, it's hard when we don't make the cut.

CUTTING THE CORD

"Parents can only give good advice or put them on the right paths, but the final forming of a person's character lies in their own hands."

—Anne Frank

I believe that we often receive messages that we aren't even aware we need until they are before us. This happened to me while on a trip to Hawaii with my family. I had many moments during this vacation where I felt apprehensive about my girls and the big decisions they were making. I was excited for them and scared at the same time. The idea of transitioning into this new phase had me struggling and feeling stuck in a place that didn't feel very comfortable. Then we stumbled upon this family from Oregon.

This beautiful family consisted of a mom and her 30, 35 and 40-year-old daughters. They were hilarious,

and they were there for the second year in a row celebrating birthdays. One night I was listening to the mom
talk to her 30-year-old daughter about not being able to
reach her the night before on her phone and how she
was worried about her. The conversation went like this:

Mom: "I was worried about you last night. I woke up
and you weren't in the house."

Daughter: "Oh, sorry."

Mom: "Well, I tried to call you and your phone was
dead as usual and you didn't say where you were going
last night. Your sisters were already asleep..."

*I would like to insert here that this was a very quiet,
calm, peaceful discussion that was happening. No
arguing, blaming or anger on either side.*

Daughter: "Sorry, Mom. I was just out walking and
didn't even have my phone with me."

Mom: "It's funny, I was really worried imagining all the
things that could happen to you. I remembered all of
the things I did when I was your age and you are a lot
like me. I figured you might be in the ocean swimming
by yourself. Then I was really concerned...but then I

thought if that is how you are going to go down there is nothing I could do about it. It kind of brought me peace when I thought of it that way. Then I was able to go back to sleep."

Daughter: "Hmm, well I am glad you went back to sleep. I'll try to remember to charge my phone."

And that was it.

There comes a time as parents and as human beings walking this earth that we realize we are not in charge, and worrying has never helped anyone.

SURRENDERING

*"Surrender to what is. Let go of what
was. Have faith in what will be."*

—Sonia Ricotti

'Ve been committed to seriously simplifying my life.
For me, that's largely been devoted to purging my
home of things I don't need and can live without.

Initially, it was difficult to part with things like certain clothes, gifts, and especially books. I've long had
an attachment to books and giving them up was something I have always been resistant to do.

But once I started with the little things it got easier.
Ironically, I had to buy a book about getting through
clutter that helped me release them. (I kept that one.)

After a few loads off to the Salvation Army I didn't
even miss what I'd donated. More and more, I just
wanted to let things go. It used to be a white-knuckled

process but I found myself, on some days, just looking for things that I could pack up and move out. Then I came across a rather large cache of old journals. I could hear myself slam on the energetic brakes.

When I looked at them, I remembered a therapist friend once suggest not re-reading old journals because you take in that old pain, angst, and trauma anew. When I came upon these journals I felt like this would be pivotal... and scary.

These journals represented phases of my life, old wounds and stories that accompany long-healed scars. These journals were physical manifestations of earlier versions of myself. And to be honest, I don't want to re-visit much of that. Growing up, and not just in my teen years, has been largely an uneven and graceless process.

So why did getting rid of these journals feel like such a stumbling block? I was starting to think it was all about surrender. Then a couple days later I got my weekly Yoga Journal email and the subject line was "Surrender" and I knew there was a lesson rolling around just waiting to land in my lap. Like all my life lessons, I let this one sit in my inbox for a few days. Did I mention I was a resister?

Blissfully, in this case, there wasn't anything to re-sist. This divine message enlightened me about the con-cept of Ishvara Pranidhana: heartfulness practice. It's the practice of releasing anything that gets in the way of aligning with the grace of being alive. A sacred shift.

I see surrender like that, too. It's a process that allows us to move forward, not always easily, but move all the same. Some things we hang onto make us better—keep us true to ourselves—and others merely keep us bound to the past and at a distance from our truth. It only makes sense that letting go of these journals was big.

It came down to this:

Am I willing to surrender who I was, who I have been, to pave the way for who I am becoming?

Am I willing to move forward, untethered, with heartfulness?

Surrender = progress.

HAVE YOU SEEN MY PADDLES?

"O' Great Spirit, help me always to speak the truth quietly, to listen with an open mind when others speak, and to remember the peace that may be found in silence."

—Cherokee Prayer

As I look back on my life, I feel as if I have spent a lot of time in what seems like neutral. And to me, sitting still doesn't feel productive most of the time. It feels like the marrow of life is dripping onto the floor without even a second glance. That might sound a bit dramatic, but all of those times I sat there, I was anxious to get moving, to do something; anything. Instead I continued to be up a creek without my proverbial paddle.

I could not throw myself into anything, including the frigid waters in which I was floating in my one woman, neutral, paddleless boat!

Can you relate?

During one of these periods of transition I sat still for what felt like months and all I could think about was cutting the mooring rope and stealing a paddle from anyone who wasn't looking. But I couldn't move. I knew what I was supposed to do. I was in transition. For the love of God, I was supposed to move on. It shouldn't have been that difficult...but it was.

For me, this particular transition was centered around my ever-changing role as mom. In a matter of a few months everything looked different. I had two children out of the house but there were still needs from afar. Psychoanalysis—I mean mothering—remotely was hard on the heart. I couldn't see their faces, but I could feel their joy and pain. The pain stuck with me. The not so funny thing is that often I would continue to feel the pangs of their sadness long after they had moved on. I kept trying to catch a current in the stream of life, searching for my paddle and yet there I sat, virtually motionless.

I thought when they all returned for the holidays and I could see their faces, hug them, sit and talk with them, that I would feel better. I was wrong. Somewhere in Boulder and in Nashville my girls jumped ship. Yes, they still needed me, but they weren't going in the same direction. They had their own choices to make, their own consequences to deal with, and wouldn't you know it...they had their own damn paddles!

So, there I was sitting in the middle of the creek floating. It turned out that I needed to sit still and let my heart catch up with my life. And once I felt my heart and life sitting together in the boat, I realized maybe the time for moving was perhaps upon me. Slowly, begrudgingly, kind of annoyed, and a little excited, I put my hands in the water to see if I could paddle my way upstream. Maybe I was ready to move, after all. Maybe I didn't need a paddle. Maybe there was a different way.

THE DASH

*"Infuse your life with action. Don't wait for it to happen.
Make it happen. Make your own future. Make your own
hope. Make your own love. And whatever your beliefs, honor
your creator, not by passively waiting for grace to come down
from upon high, but by doing what you can to make grace
happen... yourself, right now, right down here on Earth."*

—Bradley Whitford

The beauty of my job is that I meet and get to know random souls all day long. I am invited into people's lives, sometimes their homes, and I get to hear their story. I learn where they're from, who they are, and where they want to go.

It's a privilege to bear witness.

One of the amazing people I work with was born in Vietnam and she came to the U.S. when she was 13. She and her family left the day before the fall of Saigon. It's almost as if she's lived two lives in one.

Her perspective on how she wants to be in this world is remarkable. She is living what many would consider the American dream. She's built a life, her own successful business, and there really is no end to what she wants to accomplish.

I enjoy our conversations about her innovative work as a massage therapist immensely, but it's her intention in life that's humbling. She wants to be of service. She is an instrument of good. She is a healer. Above all she wants to help.

She told me her mother-in-law always used to ask, what are you doing for your dash today?

Dash?

I was confused, but thoroughly intrigued because I knew what was to follow would be fantastic. And it was. Her mother-in-law was referring to life. The dash is the line between the day you are born and the day you die.

"You only get one chance at this life, so what are you going to do?" she asked. She posed this almost rhetorically, but it felt like it was a challenge, a call to action for me, too.

This was not one of those moments that you need the passage of time to appreciate. Even as I was walking to my car, the question was swirling around in my head:

What am I doing for my dash?

My dash is a work in progress, but I am striving for it to be full, long, and a service to others.

It's a constant reminder that the arrival at your destination is far less interesting than the route you took to get there. The dash is in the living.

PART 6

ARE
WE THERE
YET?

*"All this time I was finding myself.
And I didn't know I was lost."*

—Aloe Blacc

SEARCHING FOR MEANING IN A PUMPKIN PIE

*"The trouble with jogging is that by the time you realize
you're not in shape for it, it's too far to walk back."*

—Franklin Jones

L owi and I have been off and on runners since our
teen years and I'm actually not sure what drew us
to the sport since neither of us are all that athletically
gifted. It might have been the simplicity of it all: Have
shoes. Can run.

(The second part is still a little iffy, but we have always had the shoes.)

Of course, we could gather a séance, contact Freud,
and have him reveal the deep-seated motivations for
our running and walking adventures, but we much pre-

fer to keep it simple. We are food driven. We like to eat, and if you run far, theoretically, you get to eat big.

It's not always clear when it comes to one of our adventures if we have something to prove.

What is clear is that we don't fit the usual bill when it comes to these events.

Uber-fit? Umm, no.

Genetically blessed? Aah, no.

Brave? Not generally.

A good start already. You can smell success from here, can't you?

I like to consider it a blend of stupidity and hope in the search of aliveness. Intense races scare me—intensely. It's a lie-awake-kicking-yourself-all-night-long-for-signing-up brand of scared. And yet, the insanity continues because the high at the finish line feels amazing. OK, there's a possibility that I'm confusing delirium with amazing. Often I am confused. In truth, I can't be trusted.

One of our first misguided adventures was instigated by the chance for free pie. Pumpkin pie in particular. Yes, the promise of pumpkin pie can make a girl do crazy things, like pay good money to run five miles on Thanksgiving morning. It's not like we wouldn't have pumpkin pie at our family meal. We are not in danger of not having enough food. And yet we found ourselves,

48 hours before my wedding, standing out in the cold, ready to run five miles for a pie we didn't really need.

The results of this race should've been an indication of things to come:

We were nearly last.

We were very slow.

We were poorly trained.

AND we didn't get a pie.

While what I remember most about this race is the absence of pie, it was also the beginning of what would become a long journey of upping the physical ante, if you will. Who knew that one five-mile run would lead to so many other running antics in the future? Each joint adventure from here on out would increase in mileage, physical stamina, and great joy and happiness. And after this first adventure, it was going to take way more than the promise of pumpkin pie to get us out there. It was going to take the promise of deep, soul-changing transformation. We just didn't know it yet.

LOWI
&G

TWO NIGHTS AND THREE DAYS...
WHAT'S YOUR LIMIT?

"The only way to define your limits is by going beyond them."

—Arthur Clarke

Since the Pumpkin Pie run went so well, I thought G and I should do an epic adventure. Something BIG and life changing. Not like camping along the Amazon and finding out you have blood-sucking leeches in your underwear kind of adventure, perhaps a little less than that, but bigger than five miles.

Then I found the Avon 3-Day. The race consisted of 60 miles spread over three days from Fort Collins to Boulder, Colorado. As a bonus this event was also for a good cause. During our training we would be raising money for breast cancer research. It sounded like a win-win! I immediately called G and made camping on football fields and doing 60 miles sound sexy because, hello, it is. I mean when you were in high school didn't you dream of pitching a tent and sleeping in the end zone? No? Well, apparently you didn't grow up living the real life Friday Night Lights.

Anyway, it didn't take much arm twisting. Maybe she thought something else was happening in the end zone, I can't say for sure. As luck would have it though, I was also able to convince two other Colorado friends to train for this event as well. I have always believed there is power in numbers.

After months—and I do mean months—the day came for us to begin our walk from Fort Collins to Boulder. After much fanfare all four of us began the journey together, but with thousands of participants and our differing paces we decided to keep just one partner in our sights. To say it was hot would be an understatement of monumental proportions. I am talking the kind of heat that causes a rash on your legs that doesn't go away for over a month. But I don't want to get ahead of myself because there are so many other sordid details about this epic adventure that I would hate for you to miss.

So the premise was that we were to walk 20 miles each day. Piece of cake. What they neglected to tell us was that we could not begin each day until 8:00 a.m. and if we made it to the lunch check-in prior to the prescribed time, we had to wait. What this means in layman's terms is that it took us all damn day to walk 20 miles and no amount of kiddie pools, water, and Gatorade could make up for walking in what I can only assume is the same temperature as hell. This also leads to a very full triage van hauling the dehydrated, heat-exhausted, and altitude sick souls back to the next overnight destination for IVs. Please keep in mind that this is still Day One!

Upon staggering into the finish we thought we had discovered the pot of gold. Kind of. Alongside the end zone was a semi-truck full of showers. Now if you have never experienced stall showers in a semi in 100-degree temperatures then you really haven't lived. I will also say, don't bother because when you are finished you will need another shower. After dinner and plenty of fluids it was time to assemble our accommodations for the night. We retrieved our tent and sleeping gear from the truck. Looking back on it now, putting that tent up may very well have been the last time G and I laughed together during this adventure.

After a very long night sleeping on the ground and having to pee 45 times, we woke up wet! The dew had seeped through our tent and onto our sleeping bags. Yep, this camping in the end zone was way less sexy than I had imagined—and G? Well, G was a little less than enthused with me at this point and she was feeling a little nauseous. It was already very hot as we awaited the 8:00 a.m. start. The day was not looking up as G continued to battle nausea and another one of our foursome was struggling to continue with crippling blisters.

I tried to rally G and push more fluids. I feared she was struggling with the altitude as she was as well-trained as me, if not more. I knew if this was the case that only rest, air conditioning, and perhaps an IV were going to alleviate her symptoms. The only option available was an IV and they seemed to be saving those for the poor souls who fell face first on the ground or could no longer put words together.

At lunch, I remember trying to get G to eat, but she could no longer stomach food of any kind. As I changed my socks and wrapped wet bandanas around my calves to ward off the blistering heat the realization that G could not go on began to weigh on me. I was worried and I was sad, but I knew she couldn't last much longer in this heat. I can't say how many miles we made it before G ultimately made the decision to flag the van down and go back to camp, but she was not well. Nor was she pleased with the situation.

By the end of Day Two, three of the four of us who began this adventure together were in the triage tent. I literally walked around camp for hours hydrating and checking on G. I ate my spaghetti in tears and solitude and prayed that Day Three would bring a dry sleeping bag, appetites and relief from the nausea. The night was long and, honestly, I didn't even know what to say to G at this point. She was suffering and here we were in a tent, in the middle of a football field listening to the slamming porta potty doors all night. Not cool. Not sexy. Not fun.

Day Three began slowly with the blazing heat and an inability for any of us to eat. One member of our foursome decided her feet could no longer make it a third day. Her blisters were multiplying and she could not imagine putting her shoes on, let alone walking. G could not overcome the multitude of ailments that were plaguing her and decided to meet me in Boulder. This left two of us to battle the elements for our third and final day.

It was a long, mentally challenging 20 miles. There were laughter, tears, encouragement, rest, fluids, blisters, and many concerns about how the others were doing. In the mid-afternoon heat, two of us made it across the finish line with tears streaming down our faces and a mixture of pride and sadness in our hearts. I found G lying on a cot in the field house waiting to go home. It's hard to feel accomplishment when your partner in crime, the one you convinced to do this crazy adventure, is suffering. After the pomp and circumstance at the finish we still had a long drive home. I can still remember sitting in the air conditioned car, happy to be out of the heat, but physically ill. It would take days before our appetites returned and we could eat and drink normally again. The red, swollen, itchy heat rash on our legs lasted for many weeks.

NOTHING SAYS ACCOMPLISHMENT LIKE THE SKIN OF A LEPER!

While we have done many races over the years I don't think anything has ever come close to the sustained grueling nature of this event. It still sits at the top of the heap for one of the most difficult things I have ever done. It allowed me a glimpse into what I was capable of doing if I pushed myself. I feel fortunate to have had this experience and to have made it to the other side of the finish line. On this particular day I was able to say I did it.

THREE DAYS TO MY LIMIT

"But you haven't tested your limit until you've tried something you can't do. Then you know where your limit is. It's right there where I quit. That was it. That was the limit."

—Lazarus Lake, RD of The Barkley Marathons

Upon reflection, I owe the Avon 3-Day Race a thank you. It may seem like you are experiencing deja vu right now. Lowi did just tell you all about her three-day experience but since we spent 90% of it not together, trust it's a whole new telling of other ways you can be miserable and not walk much at all.

Without banging right up against this boundary of ability, I maybe never would've learned to push harder.

Lowi invited me to do this three-day walk in which we were to cover 60 miles total, roughly 20 miles a day. It was all walking, how bad could it be?

We started Day One full of excitement, pomp and circumstance. There were several breast cancer survivors being honored as it was a fundraiser to fight this disease. After a rousing celebration of these amazing women, we were off.

Our first day's walk went fairly well. We finished in the daylight hours, which is always a sign of success to me. While Colorado is known for being dry and it is, let's be clear—it was HOT.

Hindsight being the omniscient seer, I now know I was already in trouble, but ignorance being blissful and all I was still in the dark.

I got back to camp that afternoon and I felt exhausted almost groggy. I drank water, Gatorade and even a Diet Pepsi thinking the caffeine might perk me up. No help. But I went to bed hopeful that Day Two would start with fresh energy and resolve. It did, at first.

Before long I was feeling nauseous so I took a pit stop at the aid tent. I got a quick check up and was told I was OK. The nausea continued and by our lunch stop I was falling apart. I couldn't eat, which never goes well.

Then the wheels came off and they didn't go one at a time. They all fell off all at once. And into the sag wagon I went. The sag wagon is where endurance event dreams go to die. Yes it's air conditioned and there are snacks but when you're sick, disappointed, and sweaty it's really just like being in a sad stink box.

But when I got back to camp the climate-controlled environment ended. And every time I started feeling better I would eat and I was sick again. I returned to the aid tent time and again only to hear that I was fine. But I was not fine.

I laid down in the grass that night and called my husband (the beauty of cell phones). I cried and told him that I wasn't OK and yet nobody seemed to be able to help me. He assured me I'd be fine and told me to call him when it was over the next day. I gathered myself up and headed back to my tent, but sadly I left my brand new Oakley sunglasses resting in the grass. Insult and injury added.

On Day Three, I didn't even attempt to go out and yet the altitude was still lording its dominance over me. All the sag wagon losers such as myself waited in a nice steamy gymnasium on the University of Colorado campus for most of the day. Eventually the tougher participants finishing the three-day event started to roll in, including Lowi.

I was truly so sick by this point, she found me lying on a cot telling yet another person how sick I was. The race was over, but finally I had someone telling me it was likely a combination of altitude, heat, and probably dehydration given the fact that I am an Ohioan a.k.a. flatlander. (I heard sissy, but whatever.)

My family put me in an air-conditioned car and took me back to Lowi's house. I was so happy to be back in a house and a bed. I continued to struggle eating without feeling sick even after I returned home. It was an epic fail for me. I really had trained hard for this event, but I was no match for the elements.

I felt so out of control of my own body. I kept thinking during the event if I rested I'd get better, ate more I'd get better, and I just kept feeling worse. If you ask me today I'd tell you it took me a while to get over it. But, in the deep, dark, bare-your-soul kind of honesty, I still haven't.

It was crushing for me and terrifying. I'd never had an experience like that. I felt helpless and scared. I felt bad for my sister slugging it out every day and simultaneously wondering what my problem was. There's something ominous about lying in a tent, on a football field in Who-Knows-Where, Colorado thinking, "I've never been so sick in my life and everyone is telling me I'm fine." At different points I would've begged for an IV thinking that would cure me. Maybe it would have. Maybe not.

What a fire starter disappointment can be. It was my first DNF (did not finish), although not my last. It was my first time meeting my limit and I didn't like it.

I had to come home and tell everyone I didn't finish. And that felt like failure. Nobody said that and likely nobody even cared but I did—I do. I hadn't yet learned the art of suffering. I hadn't yet heard sometimes you have to "embrace the suck." And RFM (relentless forward motion) was far from meeting my consciousness. But DNF, failure to reach the finish, that would be my teacher—again and again.

IT ALL STARTED WITH A SANGRIA

*"Continuous effort—not strength or intelligence—is
the key to unlocking our potential."*

—Liane Cardes

When someone plies you with alcohol prior to asking you something really big, you should run! Of course, in my case running is exactly what G was hoping I would do.

Approximately two years before her 40th birthday, G started tossing around the idea of a big, epic run to celebrate the occasion. She actually threw out the idea of running 40 miles! In fact, she took me to lunch and asked me what I thought about the idea. Having the three-day, a couple of marathons, and a few sangrias under my belt I thought it sounded fabulous.

Six months prior to the actual run I had committed to that fateful day, 40 miles sounded more than a little daunting. It was around this time that G decided 40 miles wasn't going to cut it. She had already accomplished that goal and now wanted more. For some people it's just never enough.

So, this is how I found myself four months prior to an event I agreed to many moons before training in the snowy, harsh conditions of a Colorado winter to run 50 miles. As an added bonus though, G and I finally convinced two of our best friends to also sign up for this adventure. We are nothing if not persuasive. I did, however, continue to ask myself weekly why G couldn't celebrate her birthday with margaritas like the rest of us 40-somethings, but she insisted it would be worth it.

Having started my training at about six months out, I was running four or five days per week and only logging about 25 miles. At the four-month mark it was time to really start upping the weekly mileage and getting the long runs done. My first set of back to back long runs were 12 and 10 miles, respectively, on the dreaded treadmill. The snow was relentless and I just couldn't weather the conditions outside as much as I hated the treadmill. The 12 miles felt awesome, but the 10? Not so much, and that is when the hunger and exhaustion started to become my weekly companion. According to G though, training through the hunger and exhaustion is the best preparation for an ultra. While this wasn't my first indication that something may be seriously wrong with G, it was a big one.

At this point I began hydrating more than I thought possible and eating more in hopes of regaining some much-needed energy.

Just when I was feeling down about my training and my lack of energy one of my friends sent me this message:

> *"I just read your blog and I realized I have not been a very good friend. I have not been supporting you in your endeavors and you are working so hard. So, in support of your training I want you to know that I, too, will be increasing my fluid intake although it will be in the form of alcohol and I will definitely be increasing my food intake. Oh, and I am not planning on running at all!"*
> *—Gina L.*

With these kind of supportive friends I knew I could make it through anything!

Most of the winter I had been splitting my time between home (where the treadmill is located) and the mountains as my daughter was ski racing. With snow up to my calves and having to wear boots, you can imagine that these were less than desirable conditions when it comes to training for long-distance running. I used the opportunity to hike up and down the ski hills multiple times a day to try and make up for the mileage I was losing. I was also praying that the 8,500 foot elevation gain was going to benefit me at sea level.

At about eight weeks out I ran 16 miles. While this was not the furthest I had ever run in my life (remember I had already run two marathons) all I could think was that, "50 is going to be a long, long...*long* way."

THE RACE GETS IN YOUR HEAD

*"One run can change your day,
many runs can change your life."*

—Anonymous

D eep into winter I was tired of the snow, freezing temperatures, and the wind. I was also very sick of the treadmill. On one particular Saturday afternoon I decided I didn't care how cold, snowy or windy it was, I was going to the trail. Heading north on the trail was great, not too cold (even though it was 18 degrees), and I liked being out there with a little light snow.

The way back was another story...

The wind was in my face, the snow was in my face, and I could no longer feel my legs. So, after almost seven miles I drove home and ran on the treadmill...again.

This was also about the time that I began dreaming about the 50 miles. I was reading the course description and I saw that there would be an elevation gain of 400 feet. So in my slumber I dreamt that we had an elevation gain the size of Mt. Everest **each and every mile!** You can imagine my relief when I awoke and realized it was just a **NIGHTMARE.**

As spring began to emerge, the weather started to improve some weeks and I managed to get a lot of runs in outside, which was a huge improvement to my mental game. Although, when the snow begins to melt you are left with the mud. I know you are beginning to see there isn't much that would make me happy right now. The sun, while a welcome sight also left me excited and unprepared one Sunday. I guess I was so excited about the warmth of the sunshine that I forgot my sunscreen. I always wear sunscreen.

Did I mention it was really sunny? Like not a cloud in the sky? I didn't even realize my mistake until I showered. Yep, it was early spring and I was fried from head to ankle!

Seriously folks, at this point in the game this whole running thing was really beginning to take its toll on all four of us who were training for the race. It was starting to mess with our heads. We were all just ready for the race to get here. When I say ready, I mean ready for it to be over. Some days I thought I could endure anything even if I had to walk the majority of it. Other days, I was not convinced I could even do a quarter of it! So, with just over a month to go I was contemplating what I was really made of.

At about five weeks from the race, I started to freak out. I was having a hard time finding my mojo. I was logging a lot of miles, being very disciplined, and now I just wanted it to end.

Every time I talked to G she kept giving me the mantra **Relentless Forward Motion.** She said it was for my benefit, but I think she needed it as much as I did at that point. It was working and kept me motivated so I wasn't complaining.

On the home front, the lack of clean clothes, food, and a path to walk through the house started to catch up with me, too. When my husband would come home and ask me what I had done that day, he didn't seem impressed that I spent several hours running, took a shower and did some laundry. I, on the other hand, was always glad I finished that much before the kids arrived home!

At the two-week mark, I got the kids off to school, did a load of laundry, picked up the house, met with a client, and then went to the trail to embark on **20 miles.** This was my last long run before the event, and I was excited. I was prepared and had snacks and extra water in the car. My plan was to run south for five miles and then back to the car for refueling and then north for five and back.

Everything went really well until about mile nine. That is when a very nice cyclist let me know that I had dropped one of my bottles about a mile back. He wasn't sure whom it belonged to until he saw me with my three bottles and one empty slot. He kindly offered to go back, but I made the decision that I would refuel and just go back the same way.

At mile 10 I was feeling good. At mile 13, I wanted to cry. My iPhone battery apparently could not handle the mileage tracker and the music and my phone was dead. Fortunately, I had already been down this path so I knew where I needed to turn around to complete my miles.

At mile 16 I needed a bathroom break and having managed it quite well earlier in the woods I thought, no problem. At this point in my journey the air force cadets were flying quite low and finding a tree with leaves in April proved challenging. I found what I thought was the perfect spot. That is until I came out of the trees, ran about a minute and then two bikers passed me with really big smiles on their faces. I am pretty sure they saw me peeing in the woods.

At about mile 17, I considered lying down on the side of the trail for a nap and waiting for my family to find me. But, alas my phone was dead and therefore my GPS was dead. The coyotes would find me before my family.

I did manage to complete my 20 miles. Then I drove home, changed clothes, ate a banana, and promptly drove to the carpool lane for after school pick up. *This full-time mom thing was really starting to get in the way of my training.*

I still wasn't sure if I was ready for 50, but I was ready for it to get here.

50 THOUGHTS FOR 50 MILES

"All it takes is all you got."

—Marc Davis

As race day loomed near, I had many thoughts and emotions that became ever present in my mind and in my heart. The list outlined below just begins to scratch the surface on what I thought each and every day from the time I opened my eyes in the morning until I closed my eyes at night.

1. I feel motivated and energized.

2. I am so tired.

3. I can't possibly run 50 miles.

4. Of course, I can run 50 miles.

5. I hope it's not windy.

6. I hope there is a slight breeze.

7. Do you think it will be warm?

8. I hope it doesn't rain.

9. Are you insane?

10. I can do this...maybe.

11. There is no way I can do this.

12. I will just do what I can.

13. I got this.

14. Long run today...or maybe tomorrow?

15. I can walk 50 miles, right?

16. I can run more when I have other people with me.

17. After my 16 mile run...I can't imagine taking another step. How am I going to do 50?

18. The altitude training is going to help me during this race.

19. It's nice out, but I really want to watch Netflix so I am going to run on the treadmill.

20. I can't possibly do another run on the treadmill.

21. I hope it doesn't snow.

22. What was I thinking signing up for this craziness?

23. I am going to walk, walking is good.

24. I am going to run as far as I can.

25. I am only going to walk for 1 minute...or 5.

26. I am not going to walk at all...ha!

27. I have to eat how much?

28. My knee hurts.

29. My feet hurt.

30. My head hurts.

31. I am starving.

32. I couldn't possibly eat anything.

33. I think I am going to throw up.

34. I threw up.

35. How long do I have to get to 50 miles?

36. Is there a drive thru along the trail?

37. Can I take a nap during the race?

38. I need how many pairs of shoes?

39. Do you think five miles at altitude equals 10 miles at sea level?

40. Is it time to taper?

41. Are we done yet?

42. How much longer?

43. If you change your mind and want to drink margaritas in the hotel…I'm down with that.

44. Wait, I agreed to do what?

45. I am all in!

46. I don't know if I have what it takes.

47. I won't quit!

48. This is going to change my life.

49. I am changing my life!

50. WE GOT THIS!

I know this list seems trivial and as I peruse it I, too, feel like it doesn't quite encompass what I was actually feeling as I prepared for 50 miles. I mean, just uttering the words 50 miles seems ridiculous. Who in their right mind even entertains the idea of running 50 miles in one day? The only thing I had to compare it to was the three-day event in which we walked a total of 60 miles and the two marathons I had done. All of these things were far from easy and they had occurred years prior and let's just say nobody was going to mistake me for a 30-something anymore!

So what was I really thinking? I was hoping and praying that my body could actually go that far. I was terrified, nauseous, I felt physically unprepared, like

a mental weenie and yet as crazy as it sounds I truly believed without a doubt that I could do 50 miles.
I have no sane explanation for why I felt this way as
the furthest I had trained was 20 miles and it did not
feel good. I just believed that barring any catastrophic
events like severe weather, illness or injury that I could
accomplish this goal. Perhaps I was being naive since I
really didn't know what to expect, but I do believe that
the mind is a powerful tool.

Days away from the Outrun 24 Hour Trail Race I
was a mixed bag of emotions. I was a little anxious, but
mostly about getting everything ready and packed and
not so much about the event. I was emotional thinking
about being with my sister and friends and working toward our goal of 50 miles. The people were what made
this worth it for me. When I visualized it we were running, laughing, and enjoying the spirit of why we came
together to do the race. That gave me a sense of excitement and peace.

When I thought about the race I wanted to be present for every second of our time together whatever
came our way. I wanted to be satisfied at the end of the
24 hours that we came, conquered, and did the best we
could on that particular day. I hoped that our best was
50, but at the end of the day I didn't know what the
mileage would add up to. I knew we might be slow, but
we are a stubborn group. When we decide to do some-

thing it's difficult to convince us otherwise. I knew we wouldn't want to stop until we reached 50.

So I rested in the knowledge that, ready or not, we were in this together.

LOWI
& G

ONE BAD APPLE
CAN LEAD TO EPIC IDEAS

"I salute the light within your eyes where the whole universe dwells. For when you are at that center within you and I am at that place within me, we shall be one."

—Chief Crazy Horse, Oglala Sioux, 1877

When you are training for your first 50-mile event, there are lots of firsts along the way.

First time training at night.

First time training at longer distances.

First time I ever had the nerve to do something that intimidated me so much.

First time I have ever been so scared and excited at the same time.

This wild, hair-brained idea began several years before it actually came to fruition. Early on in my ultrarunning endeavors I read about a runner who every year on his birthday ran his age in miles. Now this guy was 12 years old so it's not that big of a deal. (OK he was in his 20s, but still.) I, on the other hand, was already well into my 30s. I thought it sounded like an interesting and fun way to celebrate my 40th birthday.

You might already be thinking, umm, what? Why does that sound fun? I don't mean fun in its usual sense. I mean fun as in memorable, epic, outrageous, and life-changing. I thought it would change me for the better.

It's like when I read a quote from Jenn Shelton, a well-known ultrarunner: "I thought if you could run 100 miles you'd be in this Zen state. You'd be the Buddha, bringing peace and a smile to the world. It didn't work in my case. I'm the same old punk-ass as before, but there's always hope."

I was hoping it would be a confidence builder for me. I ignored the last sentence but as you probably already guessed I, too, am the same old punk.

Before long I was thinking about where this 40 miles would take place in order to celebrate my 40th birthday.

Then I went to Bad Apple Ultra 12-Hour Race. This race was a turning point for me. Up to this point, I hadn't proven myself very good at navigating physical and mental adversity.

On this day, however, I did. I was feeling sick, my ankle hurt, my knees really hurt and I nearly crashed out from low blood sugar. But with the support of my husband, John, I made it to 40 miles.

I walked a lot of it but that didn't matter. I made it through the really low points. And I didn't quit.

My perspective changed a lot after that race. I was learning how to push through; to be OK with being uncomfortable. I could continue even when it stopped being fun, even when I wasn't sure if I wanted to.

And it's always worth it in the end.

At that moment the bar had to be pushed farther. We couldn't do 40 miles for my 40th birthday. I'd already done it. It needed it to be big. And so it became 50 even though at this point my sister had only agreed to 40 miles.

Honestly, when I first broached the topic, I thought she would just run with me as part of my crew and keep me company here and there. But somewhere along the way she got the fever, too.

The idea of pushing the limit is seductive and makes you agree to things that if you really knew what it would take, you'd sober up fast and say, no.

But that, too, is part of why you say, yes. It's sick, I know.

LOWI
&G

ARE WE STILL TRAINING?

"The will to win means nothing if you haven't the will to prepare."

—Jump Ikangaa, 1989 NYC Marathon winner

Training when you're a mere mortal, not particularly gifted athletically, and you're a wimp is just what you'd think it would be. It's long, hard, and exhausting in every way: mentally, physically, and emotionally.

And all kinds of new challenges were showing up.

For the first time ever in training, I was asking myself to run 22 miles. Even when I'd done marathons I'd never gone past 20 miles. Not even for a 50K had I trained further than that.

My husband likes to say that spectators go to running events and they get all jazzed up to run because race day is sexy. But when they get down to the reality of what it takes to get to the start line it's not nearly as exciting and that's when they lose their steam.

I'd never thought about it quite in that way, but he's right.

"Game day," if you will, always has adrenaline. A regular Saturday morning in January does not. So when you wake up on a Saturday, it's below freezing, and you know you're going to be running for hours it's sometimes tough to find your motivation.

Add onto that the fact that I decided to run 50 miles the same year of the infamous Polar Vortex. Awesome planning.

If you don't recall, that year the temperatures in Ohio (and much of the midwest) were often in the single digits for weeks, which resulted in my first 22-mile training run happening on the treadmill.

It went something like this. Twelve miles in my hamstrings were squawking like crazy. I couldn't figure out if they were sore, tight or preparing to cramp. Turns out my hamstrings decided they wanted to live elsewhere. I knew this because it felt an awful lot like they were trying to escape my body while I was using them. Not the experience you want when you still have 10 miles to go.

At mile 15, it became clear that it was time to suck it up or this training run would break me. At this point, I was starting to get how people ran hard at the end of a long race. It's called, "Dear God, let it end."

When I got up the next day to run another 10 miles, the truth of how much work this was going to be began to sink in. Each week from here was an opportunity to learn and grow as a runner. That's a nice way of saying I almost lost my mind.

Nearly every week the effort grew. I would build mileage for a few weeks and then have a recovery week with less mileage (hallelujah). As race day loomed larger so did the weekly mileage.

I arrived at marathon day. This wasn't a race, but I was slated to run 26 miles. It can be summed up in five ways:

1. Extreme fatigue.

2. Mud.

3. Duct tape.

4. Home surgery.

5. Suffering.

This training day started out with the first big thaw of the winter. It was 50 degrees, and I was out at a local metro park. With all the snowfall the last few months, you know what a 50-degree day means: mud.

When I say mud, I mean the serious, sole—and soul—sucking kind. The first 10 miles of 26 were character-testers or character-builders, at least that's what my husband calls them. I call it, "Oh my God, really?"

At mile nine, I got a break from my constant internal complaining when John joined in on the run and finished out the next 17 miles. It's a tough sell to find many people who want to run 17 miles (or even five for that matter) with you so when you get a willing participant it's such a mental boost.

After all the water and mud, halfway through I realized I was getting some pretty impressive blisters. I hadn't planned on it being so wet so I hadn't brought extra socks. I didn't have Band-aids so you do what you need to in those moments: duct tape your feet.

DUCT TAPE — THE PREFERRED BAND-AID OF ULTRARUNNERS.

I imagine you are wondering how I didn't have Band-aids but I did have duct tape at the ready. It's weird, but many ultrarunners before me have figured out that duct tape is a great tool. It stays on better than a Band-aid most of the time and it's fairly waterproof.

So that's why we always have duct tape in our gear for races. Thankfully, I had it on this training day.

Shortly after taping the suffering began. There really wasn't one cause, but instead a combined recipe of fatigue, hunger, and sheer amount of time exercising all were contributing their special suffering flavors.

By day's end it was raining and it quickly cooled off to 37 degrees. So imagine you're dressed for 50 degrees, and now you've been rained on, and the wind is picking up. What do you do? You put on your husband's golf shirt from the back of his car. While on normal occasions, I would question its state of cleanliness, in this moment it was the best thing ever.

We got through the 26 and took our tired souls home. And I did stop at 26 exactly. Earlier in the day I joked that I would do the .2 to make it a full marathon. By the time I dragged myself to 26 miles, climbing in the car seemed like far too much work.

And then came another back to back training day. Whose idea was this?

After a mix of starting Daylight Savings Time and 26 miles of muscle soreness, I rolled gingerly out of bed and contemplated my planned 10-miler. But first there was a little matter of home surgery on my blisters. I will omit the more awful details, but it involved scissors, nail clippers and hydrogen peroxide. I bandaged up my war-wounds and headed out.

It took about six miles, I am a slow learner, for me to throw in the towel. Blistered, burned out, and nearly hypoglycemic was the crushing trifecta. I left the park and went home.

This wasn't even the most ridiculous training I did. My husband, who is frankly the seed-planter to most of my worst ideas, thought a night run would be a good idea. He suggested getting used to running in the dark and later in the day would help me learn to manage the evening when you are tired and everything is telling you it's time to go to bed.

It gets worse. Since I was planning a night run and it's even tougher to find someone to run at night with you, the decision was that I would run on the treadmill, in the dark, in my basement with a headlamp.

Sheer idiocy, I assure you.

It didn't take too long to realize running at night feels, well, like running at night.

In theory, it's a great idea. In practice, stupidity.

By this point our race posse of two had grown to include our friends Mary and Jill. It's amazing that you can talk more than one person into this madness, but you can't find a training partner.

As the evening began, I got texts from my training friends and a new nickname was born quickly. At first it was Crazy Horse and then as the later hours and after midnight passed then it moved to Dark Horse. At this point while I was running they were possibly imbibing.

After these training missteps and detours it became clear race day needed to get here soon.

THE END IS NEAR

*"The greater danger for most of us lies not in setting
our aim too high and falling short; but in setting
our aim too low, and achieving our mark."*

—Michelangelo

I had about three weeks left of training before our 50-mile race and it became a necessity to get super creative with the mind games. Instead of thinking about three weeks, I broke it down into the fact that I had eight hard days left of training. You can do anything for eight days, right?

Well yes, and then the weather gets dicey once more and you find yourself doing 28 miles on the treadmill. It's a hot mess in every way possible. I watched so many episodes of 24 on Netflix that it asked me at least three times if I was still watching. I started to think that even Netflix was judging me.

It was a long—very long—morning and afternoon. It really took me all damn day. And when I was done—I was done.

Around the same time I started to have trouble with my focus. More accurately—I was bored. My training had gone on a bit too long and it was time to taper down. It had taken a lot to get to this point of training and the prolonged focus was taking its toll. I was relieved when my last long run before the race was upon me. It was 20 miles and at that point what's 20 miles?

Apparently it's tougher than you think. It was awful early on because I just didn't want to do it. At mile six, I would have gladly called it a day. But as he always does, John cajoled me into continuing and once I got to 10 miles I started to feel like I could finish. I also started to think I was losing it if "just 10 more miles" seemed reasonable. What had I done to myself? Was I ever going to be able to lounge on the sofa on a Saturday without running the bejeezus out of myself? This was alarming.

Now all that was left was the last-minute prep, packing, and praying.

Race week was upon me. I was so excited, terrified, and on the verge of vomiting all at the same time, most of the time. I convinced myself that this was perfectly normal and I shouldn't worry about it.

I had accumulated nearly 900 miles in training since I'd started this adventure.

Some would say there was some craziness sprinkled in along the way and I wouldn't disagree. I experienced the gamut of emotions and had gone through breakdowns, brutally long training runs, 40-mile weekends, and more than a little insomnia.

This, of course, often begs the questions from others and myself: Why do this?

It took me a long time to understand it myself. It's one of the reasons I really love this from Miranda Lambert's song "Automatic":

> *"Hey, whatever happened to waitin' your turn*
> *Doing it all by hand,*
> *'Cause when everything is handed to you*
> *It's only worth as much as the time put in"*

There is something powerfully attractive about working really hard to achieve a goal that's just slightly out of your grasp. There is a high that you feel when you cross the line and realize that you did it. And you remember over the last several months, weeks, and even hours and minutes that you thought you couldn't do it. But then you see that you **DID DO IT!**

That's the feeling I was and still am chasing with every race. That is what I wanted 40 years old to feel like.

50 MILES, READY OR NOT

"I'm not telling you it's going to be easy...
I'm telling you it's going to be worth it."

—Unknown

Mercifully, race day finally arrived. After all that waiting, training, and anxiety it was almost a relief to get started. In the context of 50 miles, relief was not a feeling we'd have again until the finish.

Lowi and Mary flew in from Colorado and Georgia, respectively, while Jill and I made the trip by car along with our de facto race crew chief John.

The day started off with nervousness, optimism, and a dash of "holy crap, what have we done?"

In fact, we'd been asking ourselves that question and others like it for weeks. Some of us were even raging insomniacs and anxiety ridden for 40 hours before the gun went off.

The **Outrun 24** began at 8:00 a.m. with the sun in the sky and a chill in the air. John gave an inspirational speech full of wise words and the promise to care for us until we finished or... death do us part...or something like that.

It was perfect running weather and by mile three the long sleeves were ditched and we were getting into a groove. Only 47 miles to go, which somehow sounded better than when John said 23 and a half hours left on the clock! That John, he's a real inspiration.

And before we go any further, let's say it outright: **Fifty miles is far! I mean, really far.**

But with high spirits and an appropriate amount of trepidation we were off.

As the miles ticked by and the number of times we had to climb that one stupid hill on the course decreased our enthusiasm did not waiver...not yet anyway.

Did we mention there was a hill? Well, it began as a hill, but by mile 30 someone moved our hill and replaced it with Mt. Everest. OK, this might be an exaggeration, but **IT WAS NOT THE SAME HILL!**

But we are getting ahead of ourselves.

What happened during the race? What was going through our minds? Surprisingly, not all that much.

Other than the crazy conversations that occurred amongst us, it was essentially simple. What mile were we on? What mile did we just finish? Where is John? Do I need to use the restroom? That pretty much covers it until we got further into the miles.

When you run or walk for miles it all tends to run (ha, run!) together after a while. It helps tremendously to have someone to talk to. It keeps the crazy mind at bay. When you're alone, in the woods, tired, it can get rough in that space between your ears. It's part of why the 50-miler seemed so smooth much of the time. We just jibber-jabbered about nothing, everything, admired the man biscuits, and were awed by the fitness level of those around us. We laughed, we ate PB&J until it nearly killed us, and above all kept moving.

More than anything else, at an event like this, you are present. We were in the moment. Sure there are plenty of times when you're not, but overall unlike any other time in your life, you are right here. There's no place else to be. The sun was shining, the air was breezy and cool, just like we like. And we didn't have anything else to do and anywhere else to be and that is freedom.

In the course of 16 hours and 50 miles there are, to be expected, ebbs and flows of energy. Lowi and I, having similar DNA make-up, unfortunately managed to hit our lows at the same time so that made it a little tougher.

Lowi and I had the standard nausea. I say standard because almost every long distance runner encounters it at one time or another. It's miserable. And the worst part is the solution, usually, is to eat more and that's the last thing you want to do. Mary, our speedy one, had other GI distress that plagued her for miles. Her rally at the end was all guts and commitment.

At mile 18, Lowi decided that chicken soup could be a good counterpart to all that PB&J. At mile 20 she snagged herself a cup at the aid station.

As she put it: *It tasted so good...for about one minute and then my stomach began to resist. I spent the next three miles breathing in and out slowly and trying to just keep that soup in my stomach. I remember thinking that this could be one of those catastrophic events that had crossed my mind. Vomiting on the course would not bode well for me. With the aid of some Sprite and some ginger pills I was able to keep it down, but there would be very little food in my future. I sustained myself on pretzels, water, Gatorade, and saltines for the next 30 miles!*

Similarly so, I battled nausea and had an ill-fated meeting with some seasoned potatoes. It seemed like a great idea, but then, of course, it was not. But we sisters stayed together. We amazingly had the same pace even though we only trained together virtually. We had opposite strengths that kept us running through 40 miles!

Around mile 38 we were shocked we were still running. And up until about mile 42, with the exception of our poor food choices, we were having a blast!

But as we climbed into the 40-plus mile range, the wheels started to wobble and began their slow process of falling off. It was a collective downward spiral for all.

For Lowi, it was having her mind go into overdrive:

As she put it: *Yep. That is pretty much how it went for me the last eight miles. And when I say my feet hurt I mean my feet felt like a layer of skin had been peeled back and the only thing between my bloody stumps and the ground was a layer of fiery rocks! Yep, it felt that good.*

And then at mile 47 I started to cry. These are the kind of soul-searching, gut-wrenching tears that you aren't sure will ever stop. I began to question my sanity, my stamina, my ability to actually gut out the last three miles. It was dark, cold, and I truly could only think about putting one

*foot in front of the other. John tried to distract me by telling
me about his first 50-mile race and how he wanted to cry,
but by the time he finished he didn't have any tears left. I am
not sure that I felt encouraged, but I did feel like he knew
exactly the kind of pain I was in. It's important to be understood in a moment like this. You don't need a cheerleader,
you need a quiet empathizer.*

I knew Lowi was struggling and crying, but in all
honesty I had all I could handle with my own misery.
And I could hear John talking and listening, and I knew
he could handle it. He'd talked me into the finish of
more than one race and he always knows the right
thing to say.

We crossed the finish line together in the cold, dark
hours before midnight. It's always about whether you
want it badly enough. That day, we did.

When you complete 50 miles it feels euphoric. While
that may not be apparent outwardly because you're too
tired to smile, on the inside it's a million things: Relief
that you did it; relief that you get to sit down; but also
pure excitement.

It's overwhelming, satisfying, emotional, and transformative. Transformative in a way that is difficult
to explain.

All the pain, sweat, and obstacles you managed
along the way, not just in the day, but in your training

made it all worth it. You never know how far you can go, how deep you can dig until you do.

There is something about finding out what you are capable of when you have the opportunity to choose. We have all had moments in our lives where we were faced with something we would not choose to endure. Illness, loss or difficult times test us in ways we would not choose and yet we find ourselves surviving if we are lucky.

Running 50 miles isn't just about surviving. It's about pushing yourself, testing your limits, thriving; it's about choosing a different way to be. Not everyone needs to do this. Not everyone will choose to find sunshine at the finish line of 50 miles, it's just the path we chose.

I remember running through the trees and thinking how simple life can be when we let it be simple. I was intoxicated by the simplicity in that moment. I vowed to myself to remember what that felt like; to be happy, free, and unencumbered.

> *"It is a shame to grow old without seeing the beauty and strength of which a body is capable."*
>
> —Socrates

LIVING OUTSIDE THE LINES

"Life is a one time offer, use it well."

—Anonymous

I want to drop dead. This is a long-term goal of mine. Not something I hope to have happen anytime soon certainly, but it's my goal, my plan for my last act. It may sound maudlin and depressing but I promise it's not. Lowi and I say all the time we want to live big. We don't want to merely exist or mark time. We want to L-I-V-E, for real, out loud, and make it count. Part of doing that means taking risks. Some are emotional and mental like writing this book. And others are physical like, "Wow, I'm kinda close to the crumbling cliff..."

In fact, now that I say this, I realize we need to go back a little further to understand why I want to drop dead. There is a belief, a feeling, a vibe in our family that goes something like this:

Protect.

Protect.

Protect.

Play it safe.

Come back in.

Don't go out too far.

Stay away from the edge.

Don't get overheated.

Slow down.

Wait.

Don't eat hard candy while riding in the back seat of a car.

Hold my hand.

Can't you girls just go to a movie and Bob Evans so I don't have to worry about you?

Yep, that's the constant undercurrent. It comes from love AND fear. It's a desire for everyone to be safe, nobody to get hurt, everyone stays in the fold, and everything is copacetic.

With these rules you may be safe, but you are also confined.

I couldn't always articulate it or even see it objectively. It was so ingrained into who I was I never questioned it. Before long, I was an adult telling myself:

Come back.

Stay away from the edge.

Are you sure you want to take that risk?

What's your backup plan?

I realized nothing exciting was ever going to happen in these parameters. Yes, all these guidelines and rules protected me, but they shielded me from everything indiscriminately.

In the midst of this cacophonous inner conversation, I am simultaneously married to a man who is always saying yes to adventure. And guess what, he isn't dead. He is OK, safe, and living— really living!

"I refuse to tiptoe through life only to arrive safely at death," as Scott Weber declares.

I want to use it all up. I don't care if I live forever but I do care if I only exist. I want to go out like Joy Johnson. Joy was 86 years old and a New York City marathon runner who'd completed this race 25 times as well as many others. In 2013, she completed her 7:54:41 marathon and the next day she died in her sleep. She used it all up and then went softly into that good night. As she said, she wanted to "die running." And essentially, she did.

I'm not as naturally bold as it sounds. This approach leaves me anxious. Sometimes for days or weeks at a time. I choose it over being numb.

That's why we take on these adventures. We want to feel dangerously close to our limits so we can also feel wildly alive. In this life you have to play your edge. Sometimes you get too close and you may get hurt, but if you stay too far inside the lines you may never get anything at all.

You may be wondering if this Drop-Dead Life Plan has any rules or real structure to it. Not so far other than:

Say yes more than you say no.

Do things that scare the crap out of you.

```
LOWI
&G
```

ACKNOWLEDGMENTS

We are so grateful to everyone who has supported us while writing this book. Thank you to our family and close friends who have not only laughed with us, but allowed us to write about them daily.

- Our spouses, Andy and John, for believing in us and supporting us in every crazy adventure;

- Alexandra, Sydney, and Reese who continually show us what it means to live outside the lines. Thank you for inspiring us everyday;

- Our parents who gave us our wicked sense of humor and taught us the value of hard work;

- Our sister, Lisa, who has supported us and shares our crazy stories with anyone who will listen;

- Our faithful Lowi & G followers. Without you we'd just be two sisters emailing each other funny stories.

- Heather Doyle Fraser who coached, cajoled, and edited our vision into a book. We would still be talking about writing a book and making notes on Post-its without you. Through it all, you guided us with confidence and kindness to the final destination.

- Danielle Baird who believed in our book and gave it the flair and artistry we could never have imagined. Your commitment to creating an aesthetic that illustrated our words surpassed our expectations and we are immensely grateful.

- My greatly missed feline, Parsley, who sat on my lap for nearly every word I wrote during this book adventure. She was one of the best writing buddies you could ever have.

LOWI & G

Lori Brown

Angela Miller Barton

ABOUT THE AUTHORS

Lori Brown has been wrangling the wild west of parenthood for the last 22 years. Raising three daughters with her husband, Andy, she thankfully has a degree in psychology that has helped her navigate these rough and tumble waters. Lori enjoys baking, running, reading, and occasionally dipping her toe in the world of ultra events. Lori is an ICF-certified life coach and advocate for fellow parents of children with Type 1 Diabetes. She and her family reside in Colorado.

Angela Miller Barton is a recovering journalist who now works as a personal trainer and yoga instructor, as well as a health and wellness coach. In her free time, Angela enjoys cooking, training, and participating in ultra running events with her husband. She is a rebounding rebel, a spiritual seeker, and believer that practicing gratitude changes everything. She has a master's degree in exercise science, bachelor's degree in journalism as well as various fitness credentials. Angela lives with her husband John and one frisky feline in Ohio.

In 2014, Lori and Angela who long fancied themselves sarcastic Wonder Twins sprinkled with a dusting of sunshine, started a blog called Lowi & G. You can find them writing five days a week at www.lowiandg.com.

INDEX OF ILLUSTRATIONS

For more sunshine and sarcasm, visit

LOWI AND **G**.COM